"Sleep in peace, Marguerite! Much will be forgiven, for you have greatly loved!"

-The conclusion of Alexandre Dumas's novel,
La Dame aux Camélias.

Opera Journeys™ Mini Guide Series
Opera Classics Library™ Series
Opera Journeys™ Libretto Series
A History of Opera: Milestones and Metamorphoses
Opera Classics Library Puccini Companion: the Glorious Dozen

OVER 60 TITLES AVAILABLE:

•L'Africaine •Abduction from the Seraglio •Aida • Andrea Chénier
•The Barber of Seville •La Bohème •Boris Godunov • Carmen
•Cavalleria Rusticana • Così fan tutte •Der Freischütz •Der Rosenkavalier
•Die Fledermaus •Don Carlo •Don Giovanni •Don Pasquale •The Elixir of Love
•Elektra •Eugene Onegin •Exploring Wagner's Ring •Falstaff
•La Fanciulla del West •Faust •La Fille du Régiment •Fidelio
•The Flying Dutchman •Gianni Schicchi • Hansel and Gretel
•L'Italiana in Algeri •Julius Caesar •Lohengrin
•Lucia di Lammermoor •Macbeth • Madama Butterfly •The Magic Flute
•Manon •Manon Lescaut •The Marriage of Figaro •A Masked Ball
•The Mikado •Norma •Otello •I Pagliacci •Pelléas et Mélisande
•Porgy and Bess •The Rhinegold •Rigoletto •The Ring of the Nibelung
•La Rondine •Salome •Samson and Delilah •Siegfried •La Sonnambula
•Suor Angelica •Il Tabarro •The Tales of Hoffmann •Tannhäuser •Tosca
•La Traviata •Tristan and Isolde •Il Trittico •Il Trovatore •Turandot
•Twilight of the Gods •The Valkyrie •Werther •Wozzeck

All musical notations contained herein are original transcriptions by Opera Journeys Publishing.

Discography and Videography listings represent selections by the editors. Due to numerous re-issues of recordings and videos, issuer numbers and designations have been intentionally omitted.

WEB SITE: www.operajourneys.com E MAIL: operaj@bellsouth.net

Verdi's

La Traviata

Opera Classics Library™ Series

Edited by Burton D. Fisher
Principal lecturer, *Opera Journeys Lecture Series*

Opera Journeys™ Publishing / Miami, Florida

Contents

a *Prelude........*
OPERA CLASSICS LIBRARY's
La Traviata

La Traviata, together with *Rigoletto* and *Il Trovatore*, inaugurated a new phase in Verdi's compositional style; in these operas Verdi brought to the opera stage profound human passions, subjects with intense dramatic and psychological depth. Specifically, *La Traviata* is an intimate human portrait of a woman's agonizing defeat against the forces of destiny; it is a story about spiritual values, intimate humanity, and tender emotions.

OPERA CLASSICS LIBRARY explores the greatness and magic of Verdi's poignant opera. The *Commentary and Analysis* offers pertinent biographical information about Verdi, his mind-set at the time of *La Traviata*'s composition, the genesis of the opera, its premiere and performance history, and insightful story and character analysis.

The text also contains a *Brief Story Synopsis, Principal Characters in La Traviata,* and a *Story Narrative with Music Highlight Examples,* the latter containing original music transcriptions that are interspersed appropriately within the story's dramatic exposition. In addition, the text includes a *Discography, Videography,* and a *Dictionary of Opera and Musical Terms.*

The *Libretto* has been newly translated by the Opera Journeys staff with specific emphasis on retaining a literal translation, but also with the objective to provide a faithful translation in modern and contemporary English; in this way, the substance of the drama becomes more intelligible. To enhance educational and study objectives, the *Libretto* also contains musical highlight examples interspersed within the drama's text.

The opera art form is the sum of many artistic expressions: theatrical drama, music, scenery, poetry, dance, acting and gesture. In opera, it is the composer who is the dramatist, using the emotive power of his music to express intense, human conflicts. Words evoke thought, but music provokes feelings; opera's sublime fusion of words, music and all the theatrical arts provides powerful theater, an impact on one's sensibilities that can reach into the very depths of the human soul.

Verdi's *La Traviata* is certainly a crown jewel among his glorious operatic inventions: it remains a masterpiece of the lyric theater and a tribute to the art form.

Burton D. Fisher
Editor
OPERA CLASSICS LIBRARY

La Traviata

("The Fallen Woman")

Opera in Italian in three acts

Music
by
Giuseppe Verdi

Libretto by Francesco Maria Piave,
after the novel, *La Dame aux Camélias*
by Alexandre Dumas (fils)

Premiere:
Gran Teatro La Fenice, Venice
March 1853

Commentary and Analysis

As the mid-nineteenth century unfolded, the thirty-seven year-old Giuseppe Verdi had achieved recognition as the most popular opera composer in the world: he had established himself as the foremost proponent of the great legacy of Italian opera that had been preserved by his immediate predecessors, Rossini, Bellini, and Donizetti. With Verdi, Italian opera remained the rage, and its focus on the voice remained supreme and continued to be the vital force dominating the art form.

Viewing the opera landscape at mid-century, Rossini had retired almost twenty years earlier, Bellini died in 1835, Donizetti died in 1848, the premiere of Meyerbeer's *Le Prophète* took place in 1849, and Wagner's *Lohengrin* premiered in 1850.

Between the years 1839 and 1850, Verdi composed fifteen operas. His first opera, *Oberto* (1839), indicated promise for the young, twenty-six year old budding opera composer, but his second opera, the comedy, *Un Giorno di Regno* (1840), was received with indifference and failed.

It would be Verdi's third opera, *Nabucco* (1842), that would become a sensational triumph and catapult the young composer to immediate fame and recognition. Verdi's other great successes which followed were: *I Lombardi* (1843); *Ernani* (1844); *I Due Foscari* (1844); *Giovanna d'Arco* (1845); *Alzira* (1845); *Attila* (1846); *Macbeth* (1847); *I Masnadieri* (1847); *Il Corsaro* (1848); *La Battaglia di Legnano* (1849); *Luisa Miller* (1849); and *Stiffelio* (1850). Verdi would eventually compose a total of twenty-eight operas during his illustrious career, dying in 1901 at the age of seventy-eight.

Verdi's early operas all contained an underlying theme: his patriotic mission for the liberation of his beloved Italy from the oppressive rule of both France and Austria. Verdi was temperamentally a product of the previous century's Enlightenment; as such, he was obsessed with the ideals of human freedom. Verdi used his operatic pen to sound the alarm for Italy's freedom: each of the stories within those early operas was disguised with allegory that advocated individual liberty, freedom, and independence for Italy; the suffering and struggling heroes and heroines in those early operas were metaphorically his beloved Italian compatriots.

In *Giovanna d'Arco* ("Joan of Arc" 1845), the French patriot Joan confronts the oppression of the English, her own French monarchy, and even the Church, and is eventually martyred: the heroine's plight synonymous with Italy's struggle against its own oppression. In *Nabucco* (1842), the suffering Hebrews, enslaved by Nebuchadnezzar and the Babylonians, were allegorically the Italian people themselves, similarly in bondage by foreign oppressors.

Verdi's Italian audience easily read the underlying messages he had subtly injected between the lines of his text and that he had nobly expressed through his musical language. At *Nabucco's* premiere, at the conclusion of the Hebrew slave chorus, "Va Pensiero" ("Vanish, hope!"), the audience wildly stopped the performance for fifteen minutes with inspired shouts of "Viva Italia," an explosion of nationalism that forced the authorities to assign extra police to later performances of the opera. The "Va Pensiero" chorus became the emotional and unofficial Italian "National Anthem," the musical inspiration for Italy's patriotic aspirations. Even the name V E R D I had a nationalistic, underlying meaning: homage to the great patriot which was expressed as "Viva Verdi," and also as an acronym for Italian unification; the letters V E R D I signified "Vittorio Emanuelo Re D' Italia", Italian liberation associated with the return of King Victor Emanuel.

As the 1850s unfolded, Verdi's creative genius had arrived at a turning point in terms of his artistic inspiration, evolution, and maturity. He felt satisfied that his objective for Italian independence was soon to be realized, sensing the fulfillment of Italian liberation and unification in the forthcoming "Risorgimento" (1861), that historic transformation that established Italian national independence.

Verdi now decided to abandon the heroic pathos and nationalistic themes of his early operas and began to seek more profound operatic subjects: subjects that would be bold to the extreme; subjects with greater dramatic and psychological depth; subjects that accented spiritual values, intimate humanity, and tender emotions. From this point forward, he would be ceaseless in his goal to create an expressiveness and acute delineation of the human soul that had never before been realized on the opera stage.

The year 1851 inaugurated Verdi's "middle period," a defining moment in his career in which his operas would start to contain heretofore unknown dramatic qualities and intensities, an exceptional lyricism, and a profound characterization of humanity. Verdi's creative art began a new flowering toward greater maturity. He introduced operas that would eventually become some of the best loved works ever composed for the lyric theater: *Rigoletto* (1851); *Il Trovatore* (1853); *La Traviata* (1853); *I Vespri Siciliani* (1855); *Simon Boccanegra* (1857); *Aroldo* (1857); *Un Ballo in Maschera* (1859); *La Forza del Destino* (1862); *Don Carlos* (1867); *Aida* (1871). And as he neared the twilight of his career, he continued his advance toward a greater dramatic fusion between text and music that would culminate in what some consider his greatest masterpieces integrating music and drama: *Otello* (1887), and *Falstaff* (1893).

In 1851, Verdi was approached by the management of La Fenice in Venice to write an opera to celebrate the Carnival and Lent seasons. In seeking a story source for the opera, Verdi turned to the new romanticism of the French dramatist, Victor Hugo, a writer whose *Hernani* he successfully treated in his opera *Ernani* seven years earlier (1844).

Victor Hugo's play, *Le Roi s'amuse* ("The King Has a Good Time"), was a portrayal of the libertine escapades and adventures of François I of France (1515-1547), the drama featured as its unconventional protagonist, an ugly, disillusioned, and hunchbacked court jester named Triboulet: an ambivalent and tragically repulsive character who possessed two souls; he was a physically monstrous and a morally evil, wicked personality, but simultaneously, a magnanimous, kind, gentle, and compassionate man who showered unbounded love on his daughter. Hugo's Triboulet became Verdi's title character in his opera *Rigoletto* (1851).

Two years after *Rigoletto*, Verdi composed *Il Trovatore* ("The Troubadour"), an opera based on the Spanish tragedy *El Trovador* by Antonio Garcia Gutièrrez. In this story, Verdi portrayed another bold, bizarre, and unconventional character, in the hideously ugly gypsy mother, Azucena, a half-demented woman who drives the melodrama with her monomania to avenge her martyred mother.

Like the hunchbacked, mocked, and cynical Rigoletto, the powerful persona of Azucena became the keystone of *Il Trovatore:* without Azucena's obsessive passion, the essential conflict of the opera is nonexistent. In fact, the Azucena character so dominated the original source story, that the English stage version of Gutièrrez's play was titled *The Gypsy's Vengeance*. Verdi responded by musically sculpting the character of this haggard gypsy more profoundly than any character he had brought to the stage thus far. Thus,

Azucena's two great conflicting passions drive the *Il Trovatore* plot: her maternal love for her surrogate son, Manrico, and her obsession to avenge her mother's execution.

Azucena became an entirely new figure in Verdi's female gallery which, up to this time, had never made significant use of the mezzo-soprano or contralto voice in a principal role. The introduction of Azucena in *Il Trovatore* represents the beginning in a glorious pantheon of darker Verdian female voices; the sorceress Ulrica in *Un Ballo in Maschera*, Princess Eboli in *Don Carlo*, and Princess Amneris in *Aida.*

Uncannily, Azucena is Rigoletto's counterpart. Both characters are repulsive outsiders, in many respects, shocking characters to Verdi's nineteenth century audiences who demanded beautiful heroines and handsome heroes on the stage; villains could be ugly, but they were only to be presented as secondary figures. Nevertheless, in these two characters, their shared passionate obsession for revenge becomes the mainsprings of their actions, eventually concluding in horrible tragedy: Rigoletto's revenge unwittingly brings about the death of his own daughter, Gilda, stabbed by the assassin he hired to murder his master, the Duke of Mantua; similarly, Azucena causes the death of her adored surrogate son, Manrico, first by claiming under torture by her enemy, Di Luna, that she is his mother, and secondly, and more importantly, by hiding from Di Luna the fact that he and Manrico are actually brothers.

Together, Rigoletto and Azucena are the male and female faces of revenge that become defeated: revenge that ultimately brings about fatal injustice. Both tragedies, *Rigoletto* and *Il Trovatore,* are therefore loaded with irony because both protagonists believe they are striking a blow for justice, and of course, their failure leads to horrific catastrophe. Rigoletto proclaims, "Egli è delitto, punizion so io" ("He is crime, I am punishment.") Azucena repeatedly pronounces her dying mother's demand for vengeance: "Mi vendica" ("Avenge me"). Nevertheless, in the end, both see their children lying dead, the only difference between them is that Rigoletto may live on in agony, while Azucena will surely die at the stake as did her mother.

With *Rigoletto* and *Il Trovatore,* Verdi launched his crusade to bring more intensely human personalities to the opera stage. Like Shakespeare, Verdi intended — and succeeded — in presenting new characters that would stir passions and bare the soul of humanity.

Verdi's next opera, pursuing his goal for more profound characterization, would be *La Traviata.* The story source for *La Traviata* was the novel, and later the play, by Alexandre Dumas *fils* (1824-1895), *La Dame aux Camélias* (1848) ("The Lady with the Camellias.") Dumas *fils* was the illegitimate son of the renowned Alexandre Dumas, *père,* the writer of those famous novels, *The Count of Monte Cristo, The Three Musketeers,* and hundreds of others. History records that the elder Dumas actually sued his illegitimate son for taking his name, accusing him of flagrantly capitalizing on his father's fame and success.

Dumas *fils* was for a short time the lover of the real life courtesan, Alphonsine Plessis, an extremely popular and successful demimondaine of Paris. She preferred to be called Marie Duplessis, but became Marguerite Gautier in Dumas's novel, and eventually, Verdi's heroine Violetta Valery in his opera *La Traviata.*

Dumas idealized his brief love affair with Marie Duplessis in his novel, and transformed her rejection of his passionate love for her into a tragic love story whose telling acquired almost mythological proportions. Their tempestuous affair ended because of Dumas's financial incapabilities, and Marie's infidelity.

Dumas's heroine, Marie, was born in the countryside at Nonant and was the daughter of a textile merchant who apparently abandoned his family. At the age of fifteen, she was sent to Paris, where she worked in a shop by day, but learned quickly the financial rewards of prostitution by night. Within a short time she had risen to the highest circles of the demimondaines, and was maintained as a mistress successively by dukes and counts, all of whom installed her in apartments and provided her with material luxuries.

Marie loved flowers, but because she was allergic to heavy aromas, she would wear the almost odorless white camellia. Her life was filled with paradox; as a courtesan, she would be reviled by society for her immoral life-style, but to others, she was openly admired for her beauty and respected for her presumed refinement. Franz Liszt, a patron who adored her, claimed that her wit, good sense, and elegant conversation prompted sincere respect and esteem. Likewise, Marie was captivated by Liszt; one of her greatest disappointments was that her illness prevented her from accompanying Liszt on one of his tours.

While Marie was the mistress of Count Stackelberg, an elderly former ambassador to Russia, Dumas accidentally met her while she was entertaining friends in her apartment. She began to cough blood, and Dumas followed her to her bedroom where his genuine concern for her health so touched her, that she admitted him as her lover.

Dumas could not provide her with the luxury she required, and as a result, she refused to renounce her other lovers. Their love affair became stormy, unhappy, and eventually terminated. In parting, Dumas wrote: "My dear Marie, I am not rich enough to love you as I would wish, and not poor enough to be loved as you would desire. So let us both forget..."

In his novel, Dumas poured out his spurned soul, and at the same time, idealized this woman who had caused him so much suffering, ultimately, ennobling himself as a victim of his own sentimentality and impossible dreams, but begging the reader's pity. Nevertheless, Dumas *père* was not responsible for breaking up their relationship, so the father's intervention in both novel and play (Giorgio Germont in Verdi's *La Traviata*) was a fictional creation that had no basis in the reality of Dumas's life.

Marie became ravaged by tuberculosis, and went from spa to spa to try to regain her health, but eventually, her disease accelerated to total physical decline, presumably as a result of her obsessive desire to maintain her professional life-style. Marie died from the disease in 1847. She was twenty-three years old, and the next year, Dumas published his novel.

Much of the story recounted in Dumas's *La Dame aux Camélias* mirrors another celebrated novel, the Abbé Prévost's eighteenth century autobiographical novel, *Mémoires et aventures d'un homme de qualité,* the accepted English translation, "The History of the Cavalier Des Grieux and Manon Lescaut."

Manon Lescaut, also a courtesan, became the role model for the *demimonde* society of the nineteenth-century, and the subject of operas by Auber, Puccini, and Massenet.

The Abbé's fictional Manon Lescaut was a beautiful, immoral courtesan who genuinely falls in love with a young student, des Grieux, and a man who is unable to give her the luxury she cannot do without. Eventually, she abandons her lover in order to return to her profession.

The Prévost/Dumas/Verdi stories are all related and deal with young impetuous people whose lives become destroyed because their passions overcome reason: all of the stories deal with the death of love and the tragic death of lovers.

A turning point in all of these stories concerns abandonment: a lover is abandoned for material reasons, money (Prévost), or a lover is abandoned because of a noble sacrifice (Dumas/Verdi): the former and the latter come together at the end of Act II - Scene 1 of *La Traviata* in a subtle — if not ironic — moment. When Alfredo returns, and before Giuseppe, Violetta's servant, delivers Violetta's farewell letter to Alfredo, stage instructions direct that the Abbé Prévost's novel lay opened on a table to the page containing Manon's farewell letter to her lover:

> "But can you not see, poor dear soul, that in the condition to which we are reduced, fidelity would be a foolish virtue? Do you think it possible to be loving on an empty stomach? Hunger would cause me some fatal mishap, and one day I would utter my last breath thinking it as a sigh of love........"

Nevertheless, *La Traviata's* story elevates abandonment to noble sacrifice. Sarah Bernhardt, for whom Sardou wrote the play *La Tosca* that later became the basis for Puccini's opera of the same name, recognized the suitability of Dumas's play as a vehicle for a great romantic actress: she immortalized Marguerite Gautier in *La Dame aux Camélias,* and reputedly performed the role three thousand times. An equally great actress, Eleanore Duse, performed the same role throughout Europe and America, and in contemporary times, it became a brilliant role for Greta Garbo who played the heroine in its film version: *Camille.* Nevertheless, it became the celebrated Bernhardt who coined the famous epithet for the heroine when she referred to *La Dame* as the legendary "whore with a heart of gold."

Verdi's *La Traviata* resulted from a commission to write a new opera for the 1853 Carnival season that would be mounted at the Teatro La Fenice in Venice. As his librettist, Verdi selected Francesco Maria Piave, librettist for his previous *Ernani, Macbeth, Rigoletto,* and the poet who would later become his librettist for *La Forza del Destino.*

Composer and librettist had seen a Paris production of Dumas's play, and Verdi considered it "a subject of the times." Its initial title, *Amore e morte* ("Love and Death"), would be changed to accommodate the censors: *La Traviata* ("The Fallen Woman.") They elected to base their opera on Dumas's stage play rather than his novel: the novel depicted the heroine as a rather promiscuous and crude personality, but in the play, she was portrayed as a more refined and sedate woman.

Years before *La Traviata*, Verdi wrote to a friend, "I don't like depicting prostitutes on the stage," a statement he made to defend his refusal to set Victor Hugo's *Marion de Lorme* for the opera stage. However, at this juncture in his life, Verdi was intuitively urged, sensitive, and inspired toward this subject: he was deeply moved by the poignancy of the doomed heroine's plight, a tragedy involving the abandonment of her one true love as well as the sacrifice of her life to illness. The story's dramatic events eerily paralleled Verdi's own personal relationships, and those associations served to direct him — consciously and unconsciously — toward this profoundly human story.

A creative artist seeks truth and beauty, and expresses his ideals like a philosophical barometer that measures society's pulse. Verdi admittedly was a moralist: a man who considered himself a priest, and would use his art to teach morality. Dumas's story had a very special attraction to him because it exposed immorality: therefore, it was indeed, "A story of our times." In one sense, Verdi intended his dramatization of the story to expose the exploitation of women by wealthy men, well aware that the lives of these courtesans could be heartless, loveless, and abusive, and almost always tragic when they would be cast aside when their charms faded.

There are many moments in a composer's life when life and art collide. Years earlier Verdi suffered personal tragedies with the death of his young wife, which was followed almost immediately by the death of his two children. So the tragic death of Violetta in *La Traviata* corresponded uncannily with his own personal tragedies.

In another collision of life and art, Dumas's heroine sells her jewels to pay for the expenses of the lover's country retreat. In the early years of Verdi's marriage, he became ill and was unable to pay the rent; his wife sold her jewels and paid the rent with the proceeds. And at the time of her death, Verdi's wife was young by any standard: she was twenty-seven. A further coincidence, her name was Marguerita.

Biographers speculate that the more emphatic underlying inspiration for Verdi's enthusiasm in setting *La Traviata* for the lyric stage concerned the story's parallels with his romance with Giuseppina Strepponi, a relationship that all of Italy considered scandalous. Strepponi had been a renowned opera singer who had become a guiding force in Verdi's early operatic career. She was the prima donna soprano in the premiere of his third opera, *Nabucco,* and was not only instrumental in helping the twenty-nine year-old composer have *Nabucco* produced in 1842, but afterwards became an important influence in his career.

After the death of Verdi's wife, Strepponi and Verdi fell in love. They lived together in the countryside outside Paris, their sinful love idyll hauntingly similar to Dumas's novel and play. Both became victimized by ferocious assaults of moral outrage from the genteel elements of Parisian society, their relationship considered illicit and scandalous by an adoring public who seemed to have demanded an unrealizable sainthood from their beloved opera icon. Even Verdi's esteemed former father-in-law, Antonio Barezzi, felt obliged to reproach him for what he considered his thoughtless association with Strepponi. (Verdi and Strepponi eventually married years later.)

Subsequently, Strepponi became ill and depressed. It has been speculated that much of her illness resulted from the loss of her voice; her career had been ruined from overwork and from her attempt to support and raise her two illegitimate children after their father's death. Afterwards, in desperation, it is reputed that she had lovers who fathered at least four more illegitimate children. Strepponi's past, by any measure of nineteenth century or even contemporary morality, was dark and outrageous, and it ultimately became the cause for her rejection, repudiation, and condemnation, particularly by Verdi's fellow villagers after the couple eventually settled in his native Busetto.

The immoral Strepponi was viewed by society as the "fallen woman," a woman deserving of scorn and derision, and as a result of her victimization, she suffered much pain, despair, and anguish. Nevertheless, Verdi became her loving savior and protector against a vicious and hypocritical society: it was ultimately through their profound love that Strepponi was redeemed, and her spirits restored.

It became Verdi's personal ideals of love, forgiveness, and redemption, noble ideals which he acted out in his real-life relationship with Strepponi, which became the powerful, inspirational, underlying forces that drove him toward the poignancy of Dumas's story. Verdi was determined to use his opera medium to arouse sympathy, understanding, and compassion, for society's outcasts. *Rigoletto, Il Trovatore*, and *La Traviata,* all composed within two years of each other, almost form a trilogy whose basic themes deal with society's cruelties, as well as relationships that have become disrupted by irrational passions: the ugly and corrupt Rigoletto, the demented and dangerous Azucena, and the scorned Violetta.

The collision of Verdi's life and art became the underlying inspiration for his poignant musical outpouring in *La Traviata.* It is an opera story that occupied a very special place in Verdi's sentiments and affections, and therefore, became an extremely intimate and personal expression: Violetta, the "fallen woman," rejected and doomed, was his real-life, beloved Giuseppina Strepponi, a woman whom the composer himself redeemed through unbounded love and forgiveness.

Europe's mid-nineteenth century was a time of political and social unrest. Napoleon's earlier defeat and the political alliances that evolved from the Congress of Vienna (1813-1815), had given Europe's victorious monarchies a renewed incentive to protect the status quo of their autocracies through force. The eighteenth century Enlightenment awakened humanity to democracy and individual liberty, inspiring one of the greatest transformations in human history: the French Revolution. Napoleon arose from the ashes of the Revolution and the Reign of Terror, but failed to destroy the monarchies. In the aftermath of his defeat, the monarchies felt threatened by ethnic nationalism as well as new ideological and social forces evolving from the transformations caused by the Industrial Revolution, colonialism, materialism, and socialism. More importantly, society's dreams of democracy were propelling stormy winds of change that threatened Europe's autocracies, generating fear among the monarchies that their power was vulnerable. As a result, ideals about human progress and reform were continually in tension and conflict, and revolutions, bred by discontent, erupted in 1830 and 1848 in all the major cities throughout Europe.

The control of ideas was a coefficient of power. The ability of the continental powers to control artistic truth was directly proportional to the stability and continuity of their authority. Censorship was the engine to control and regulate ideas expressed in the arts: nothing could be shown upon the stage that might in the least fan the flames of rebellion and discontent. Kings, ministers, and governments, all reflected an apparent paranoia, an irrational fear, and an almost pathological suspicion of new ideas. It was through censorship that they exerted their power and determination to protect what they considered "universal truths": in order to survive, conservatism and fundamentalism would of necessity overpower progress and new ideas.

In France, the censors suppressed Victor Hugo's play *Le Roi s'amuse,* the basis for Verdi's *Rigoletto.* Despite the French Constitution's guarantee of freedom of expression, the censors banned the play, deeming its subject immoral, obscenely trivial, scandalous, and even a subversive threat. Similarly, in Verdi's Italy, ruled by France, Austria, and the Roman Catholic Church, censors would reject and prevent the performance of works by artists whose ideas they considered a threat to the social and political stability of their regimes.

For *Rigoletto,* Verdi and Piave fought profusely with the censors who deemed its curse theme antithetical and blasphemous: the portrayal of the misdeeds and frailties of King François I was considered obscene and despicable; its plot contained political incorrectness with a king manipulated by a crippled jester, eventually becoming an intended assassination victim; its sleaziness in Sparafucile's Inn had the "aura" of a house of prostitution; and finally, it was considered repulsive when Gilda was "packed" in a sack in the opera's final moment.

Verdi would overcome their objections and substitute the Duke of Mantua for King François I, in effect, the Duke bearing the anonymity of any Mantovani, an insignificant ruler of a petty state rather than an historic King of France. But it was a stroke of operatic Providence that redeemed both Verdi and Piave: the Austrian censor himself, a man named Martello, was not only an avid opera lover, but a man who venerated the great Verdi as well. Martello determined that the change of venue from Paris to Mantua, and the renaming of the opera to *Rigoletto* from its originally intended *La Maledizione* ("The Curse"), adequately satisfied censor requirements. From the point of view of both Verdi and Piave, *Rigoletto* had returned from the censors safely, and without severe fractures or amputations.

And indeed, Verdi's *La Traviata* story prompted the censors to fury, considering the mere portrayal of a courtesan on the stage as anathema. In addition, censors considered "Libiamo," the famous drinking toast in Act I, too licentious. But it would be Alfredo's outpouring of love for Violetta in Act I that prompted the censor's outrage and condemnation of *La Traviata.* Some of the text was considered blasphemous: Alfredo's words, "Croce e delizia al cor" ("pain and ecstasy to my heart") bore another connotation; "croce" also denoted "cross," obviously a holy association in Christian Europe. Verdi was urged to change "croce" to "pena," a synonym for pain.

Verdi refused. But in the end Verdi was the victor. The opera was to premiere at La Fenice in Venice, and the Venetian censor was again none other than his passionate admirer, Martello, the savior of *Rigoletto. La Traviata* returned from the censors — like *Rigoletto* — without severe amputation, and with inconsequential changes that were far less than those he had experienced with *Rigoletto.*

Verdi's *Il Trovatore* premiered in Rome in 1853, just two months before *La Traviata's* premiere in Venice. Although seemingly written simultaneously, no two operas could possibly be so different if not antithetical: their fundamental differences in spirit, technique, and theme, certainly represent a compliment to Verdi's genius.

Perhaps one of *La Traviata's* most famous legacies is that its premiere at La Fenice in Venice in 1853 was reported to have been the most colossal operatic disaster and fiasco of all time. The public did not quite agree with Verdi about the subject's poignancy and timeliness. It was considered too avant garde, an unusual work that may have been too contemporary and too modern, and contrary to their expectations, a work with no intrigues, no duels, and none of the ornamentation of high operatic romance.

Verdi's insistence on setting the story in contemporary costume, which would emphasize "a subject of our times," may have contributed to a sense of stark, ugly realism for its audience. It would be at later performances that *La Traviata's* setting would be moved back one hundred years and be produced with the period costumes of the early eighteenth century: Louis XIV. If anything, the immorality inherent in a plot depicting the glorification of a courtesan's life was entirely too repulsive, and perhaps a little too bold for Verdi's contemporary audience.

In the mid-nineteenth century, conservatives considered the realism that was being portrayed in contemporary French literature to represent corrupting influences: those contemporary literary realists such as Stendhal and George Sand were thought to be twisting Enlightenment ideals, not merely excusing illicit love, but attacking the very institution of marriage itself; their works were considered the ultimate immorality, and *La Traviata,* a reflection of modern society, in many ways represented that immorality.

Hypocritical criticism? A veil to hide those blatant truths and realities of their society? The women in the audience plainly knew that many of their husbands maintained girlfriends, but that was not a subject to be discussed around the dinner table, and certainly far from something they wanted to face so realistically in a stage portrayal. In addition, parents who brought along their young daughters were duly appalled to have their protected youngsters witness the glorification of the heroine-courtesan Violetta in Act I successfully selling sex and ultimately wearing the most luxurious finery in the house.

But the premiere disaster had yet another dimension. The tenor had a cold and was reported to have been croaking throughout the performance. And a Mme. Fanny Salvini-Donatelli, an extremely stout and healthy looking soprano, looked anything but the beautiful and consumptive courtesan, Violetta. It became obviously difficult — if not ludicrous — for the audience to envision this monumentally hefty woman in the role of a beautiful courtesan whose consumption wastes her away to nothing.

In retrospect, *La Traviata's* momentary premiere failure was but a glitch in opera history. Today, the opera is without question one of the most widely loved operas, and perhaps the unequivocal sentimental favorite in the Verdi canon.

La Traviata is an overwhelmingly poignant portrait of a heroic woman who becomes tormented in her struggle to overcome the tragic realities of her life. In this exceptional creative outpouring, Verdi's music language ingeniously expresses her profound inner turmoil and psychological truths.

Those sentiments and human feelings expressed in *La Traviata* place it at the summit of the nineteenth century Romantic movement. For earlier Enlightenment thinkers, reason was the path to universal truth. But the Enlightenment bred the French Revolution and its ultimate horror, the Reign of Terror, and Romanticism became the counter-force — if not the backlash — to the failure of the Enlightenment. Romantics turned to Rousseau, a spiritual founding father of the Romantic movement, who championed the freedom of the human spirit when he said: "I felt before I thought."

Thus, Romantic ideals stressed profound human sensibilities, and idealized human achievement as a tension between desire and fulfillment. As a result, Romanticists ennobled love and the nature of love; they glorified sentiments and virtues; they expressed sympathy and compassion for man's foibles; they idealized death as a form of redemption, and rewarded noble acts and sacrifice.

Goethe expressed those Romantic sentiments in his *Sorrows of the Young Werther* (1774), a story in which the tragedy portrays suicide as the ultimate solution to unrequited love. Victor Hugo, in the *Hunchback of Notre Dame*, (1831), poignantly portrayed human tragedy in his portrayal of the pathetic and sad plight of the deformed Quasimodo.

In music, the Romantic spirit emphasized its liberation from Classical restrictions by eliminating rigid structural constraints, such as strict adherence to rhythms, balances, and preestablished forms. Liberated from Classicism, the Romantics portrayed their art with a freer musical expression that resulted in grandiose and extravagant musical representations: Chopin's Ballades, Impromptus, and Nocturnes, and Liszt's Symphonic Poems and Rhapsodies.

Beethoven's *Fidelio* (1805) was the first Romantic opera, an idealization of freedom from oppression in which the rescue of a political prisoner is portrayed as a thrilling ode to love and freedom, all accented with a deep sense of human struggle hammered into every note. But the icons of nineteenth-century Romanticism in opera were Giuseppe Verdi in Italy, and Richard Wagner in Germany: each composer had an agenda and mission that reflected his own contemporary vision of a more perfect world.

Wagner was the quintessential cultural pessimist who proposed that the path to human salvation could only be achieved through the sacrificing love of a woman. Goethe had ennobled woman in his ending of *Faust*: "Das Ewig-Weibliche Zieht uns hinan." (The eternal woman draws us onward.") Wagner and the German Romanticists became obsessed with the ideal of the "eternal woman": in Wagner's *The Flying Dutchman* (1843), the heroine Senta sacrifices her life to redeem the doomed Dutchman, her sacrifice serving to eliminate his curse. In Wagner's colossal *Ring* operas, it is Brünnhilde's love for the hero Siegfried that ultimately leads to her self-immolation, a sacrificial act that redeems the world from evil.

And in the dramatic truth portrayed in *La Traviata*, its deep sentiment and poignant portrait of the entire range of human feelings and emotions, Verdi represented the essence of the Romantic spirit and soul.

As an artist with high moral ideals, Verdi unveiled the human soul in *La Traviata*. Verdi was a man possessing Romantic ideals: he was an extremely compassionate and sensitive man, most assuredly a humanistic man.

Verdi believed that a single act of sin, an injustice, or an indiscretion, should not blacken a life: forgiveness, atonement, and penitence were essential redemptive forces that led to the path of personal salvation. But Verdi was a true Romantic: love was the ultimate fulfillment that would achieve redemption. Love and its redeeming power could transform and rescue an amoral life. Verdi practiced what he preached: his unbounded love for Giuseppina Strepponi was indeed the redeeming force in her life, and it was his selfless love for her that liberated her from a dark and sinful past.

Personal salvation and redemption are the core spiritual themes of *La Traviata*. The heroine, Violetta Valery, is a courtesan, a sinful woman who by her profession blasphemously confronts the moral standards of society: she is immoral and amoral. In that sense, Violetta is indeed the lost soul of the story: the "traviata," variously translated as "the woman astray," "the wayward woman," "the woman amiss," and "the fallen woman."

Nevertheless, humanity is flawed, and lives are continually threatened by duplicity and double standards. Mozart, in his operas *Don Giovanni* (1787), and *The Marriage of Figaro* (1786), portrays despicable, promiscuous, and immoral men, but if viewed in the context of morality plays in which good triumphs over evil, men must repent or be punished: an essential necessity in order to preserve humanity and society. But promiscuous women, especially courtesans, were considered beyond sympathy and certainly salvation, and they, not their consorts, became the condemned.

In the spirit of the Romantic ideal, Violetta Valery can rise above her past and can be redeemed, but she must perform a noble deed, a heroic act, a selfless sacrifice in order to earn her redemption and forgiveness. Her sacrifice is the heart of the opera story. It is a heroic moment indeed when Violetta agrees to abandon her passionate love for Alfredo for the good of his family; her sacrifice is a selfless act of true love, and the moment in which she thinks of everyone but herself. It is indeed a poignant moment, during her second act confrontation with Giorgio Germont, when Violetta reflects: "Conosca il sacrifizio ch'io consumai d'amore che sarà suo fin l'ultimo sospiro del mio cor" ("One day Alfredo should know the sacrifice I made for him, and with my last breath, I loved only him.) And a no less poignant moment of selflessness occurs later when she embraces Germont and reflects: "Tra breve ei vi fia reso, ma afflitto oltre ogni dire" ("Soon you will have him back, but he will be so brokenhearted!") These are truly moments of selflessness and noble human magnanimity.

Ultimately, Violetta's sacrifice achieves forgiveness for her sinful past, and her heroism becomes a transcendence that serves to spiritually elevate her and redeem her soul.

In so many poignant moments of the *La Traviata* story, deep psychological complexities and intense emotions build to a fierce pathos. And as the tragedy progresses, the mood develops into a deep sense of pity and sorrow. Violetta, selflessly and compassionately, has nobly and heroically sacrificed her love for Alfredo for a greater good, but in the end, her final sacrifice will be life itself. With Verdi's poignant and dramatic musical portrait of the heroine's struggles and her intense sentiments, she truly earns her epithet: "the woman with a heart of gold."

Verdi's magical and sublime music portrays the pathos and tragedy of his doomed heroine with a deep sense of dramatic realism. His score is almost a bittersweet symphonic-opera that sweeps like an emotional tide while it conveys powerful moments of emotional truth in each stage of the heroine's plight. Verdi even uses the vocal character of the heroine to arouse our consciousness of the true soul of the woman: vocally, Violetta becomes transformed from the ornamented and exuberant coloratura in Act 1, to her more lyric, dramatic, and more passionate expressiveness as she approaches her ultimate doom.

In the orchestral prelude, Verdi introduces the heroine Violetta with two heartfelt and moving musical themes that portray the entire emotional spectrum of the drama. At first, softly played on divided strings, Verdi's musical language presents a theme that conveys a profound sadness and melancholy, a reflection on the fatal illness that undermines Violetta's health and serves to evoke a sense of suffering and pain.

A second intensely moving theme relieves that pathos and sadness and announces love: Violetta's profound and devoted love for Alfredo. Verdi ends the prelude ingeniously by adding ornamentation to the love theme, a subtle musical suggestion of the shallowness and superficiality of the professional courtesan's world and its decadent salons. This is, beyond any doubt, Verdi's "story of our times," and his musical expressions from the very beginning serve to emphasize his very human moral outrage.

Violetta is quite candid, if not fearful, when she advises the impetuous Alfredo that a woman committed to her profession could never expose herself to the extravagance of a serious love affair; nevertheless, it becomes Alfredo's ardent declaration of love that unconsciously lays bare her protected inner feelings. Violetta is indeed human, and at this moment, her capacity to reason has become daunted.

In the first act, Alfredo's outpouring of love, and in particular, the refrain from his aria expressed in the words "Di quel amor" ("It is a love that throbs like the entire universe"), bears an astonishing musical resemblance to Violetta's love music first heard in the prelude. Nevertheless, Alfredo's variation is now full of verve and energy, whereas Violetta's version bears a suggestion of femininity and passiveness. Verdi obviously intended their music to be complementary, a subtly romantic idea that implies a sense of mutual dependency, and an even more subtle suggestion that these two individuals are destined for each other.

Violetta, the woman dedicated to the pursuit of pleasure, begins to function on an unconscious level: she is apparently confused, but indeed receptive and deeply moved by Alfredo's great offer of love. She has been touched by the transforming power of desire and fulfillment and is ready to give up everything: her friends, her profession, her security, and all her defenses. Although she is haunted by doubts and fears concerning her illness, she momentarily defies everything and submits herself to fate and destiny: to emotion rather than reason..

Violetta closes the first act with her aria "Sempre libera" ("Always free"), a cabaletta, in this definition, a two-part aria with fast and slow tempos intended in its style to be a dazzling display piece that shows off the singer's virtuosity. "Sempre libera" is the vocal centerpiece of the first act, if not the entire opera: the aria places excruciating demands on the singer because its florid passages rest in the highest area of the soprano's range; several sustained high Cs, as well as several short D-flats, are all embellished with a variety of trills and falling scales.

Violetta's words are ironic and are not to be taken literally. In fact, everything Violetta says during the finale of Act I means the opposite: Violetta is saying no when she means yes. Violetta is not a "free" woman as she claims, but rather, a slave to her profession and its rewards: a slave to those who maintain and possess her. In truth, Violetta is a prisoner of her life-style, and unconsciously yearns to escape from it.

So in the end, the "Sempre libera" aria contains an emotional subtext: Violetta is a woman in fear, despair, and guilt, and her presumed rejection of Alfredo seems to represent an excuse to pursue the frivolous life, but in truth, it represents no more than a disguise for her self-hatred; it is psychological denial, because after all, Violetta, like all humanity, craves and yearns for love. "Sempre libera" is Violetta's attempt to rationalize her freedom and independence, but under its surface, it expresses the emotional hysteria of a woman in deep conflict: a woman in tension between desire and fulfillment; a woman craving true love whose inner self is in conflict between emotion and reason..

Alfredo's voice is heard from offstage, or Violetta imagines she hears Alfredo's voice. Verdi is repeating his most recent tour-de-forces in which offstage voices serve to heighten the music drama: in *Il Trovatore*'s "Miserere", Leonora hears Manrico's lamenting voice from the Aliaferia prison; in *Rigoletto*, the Duke's voice is heard offstage singing "La donna è mobile," ultimately awakening Rigoletto to horrible realities.

In hearing Alfredo's voice, Violetta's resolution to remain free is challenged: an opportunity for her to repeat her refrains and add a renewed and forceful outburst to her determination to remain free; her words deny love, but in truth, her unconscious yearns for the freedom to love; this is the irony of the "Sempre libera."

The arrival to Act II is a sudden transition: almost without explanation. After Violetta's rejection of Alfredo in her Act I "Sempre libera," the scene suddenly moves to the happy idyllic life in the countryside outside Paris. The frivolous courtesan of Act I no longer exists, but rather, a happy and contented woman. However, from the beginning of Act II to the conclusion of the opera, Violetta becomes a woman in continuous conflict, cruelly tested both morally and emotionally. Verdi, the narrator of this story, tells us through his music that there is a sure sense that something will go wrong, and certainly, everything does go wrong.

Giorgio Germont, Alfredo's father, a noble, respectable, high-minded, religious and God-fearing gentleman from Provence, arrives to persuade Violetta to renounce her love for Alfredo: Alfredo's sister, "pure as an angel," whose "fiancé will refuse to marry her" if the scandalous and profane liaison of his prospective brother-in-law (Alfredo) continues.

Germont makes a terrifying presence, musically and textually, and Violetta's confrontation with him becomes a monumental battle of wills: duets that become duels. Violetta struggles, becomes agitated, and communicates in breathless sentences. At first, Violetta remains steadfast, unwilling to give up her new-found love: she pleads frantically with Germont, attempting to persuade him that she is ill, that the end of her life is near, that she has no family or friends, and that her love for Alfredo has become the essence of her life as well as her salvation.

Germont pontificates, assuring her that she will have future happiness, a reward inspired by God; she will find Heaven, her soul will be saved, she will be forgiven for her sins, and she will be redeemed. Violetta reasons — the core of the opera story — that she cannot become an obstacle and burden to Alfredo's happiness: she must accede to Germont, because if not, society will never forgive her.

Eventually, it is the elder Germont, the father who has come to challenge the courtesan for his son's sake, who develops a profound respect for the woman whose heart he must break, rather than for his own son for whose sake he has intervened. Germont's poignant "Piangi, piangi," urging Violetta to cry to relieve her emotions, represents the human side of Germont: he weeps with and for Violetta, as if she were his own daughter, ultimately developing respect and love for the woman whose heart he has come to destroy.

Every artist treads on autobiographical terrain, and Giuseppe Verdi certainly cannot be excluded. Verdi's operatic "father figures" dominate his operas. There is a certain psychological truth when those fathers and their offspring are seemingly alone in the world, as in *Rigoletto,* where a father obsessively overprotects his child, when his child seems to be threatened by an alternate man, and when the father-daughter relationship possesses an almost incestuous structure.

Verdi's relationship with his father was full of constant conflict, tension, and bitterness. He claimed that his father never seemed to have understood him, and even accused his father of jealousy and envy as he transcended his parents' social and intellectual world. As a result, Verdi was virtually estranged from his father, but within his inner self, he longed for fatherly affection and understanding. In a more tragic sense, Verdi's young daughter and son died in their childhood, preventing him from lavishing parental affection on his own children, an ideal that lies deep within the soul of Italian patriarchal traditions.

But Verdi would express the paternal affection he never had, and the paternal affection he could never give to his own children, in his own unique musical language: his operatic creations became the aftershock of those paternal relationships he lacked and yearned for in his own life.

In many of his operas, Verdi presents us with a whole gallery of passionate, eloquent, and often self-contradictory father figures, fathers who are passionately devoted to, but often in conflict with their children. Those father figures — almost always baritones or basses — present some of the greatest moments in all of Verdi's operas: fathers who gloriously pour out their feelings with floods of honest emotion and intense passion.

In *La Forza del Destino* ("The Force of Destiny"- 1865), the tragedy of the opera concerns a dying father laying a curse on his daughter Leonora, as the heroine struggles in her conflict between her love for her father versus her lover, Don Alvaro. In *Don Carlos* (1867), a terrifying old priest, the Grand Inquisitor, approves of King Philip II's intent to consign his son to death, the father agonizing and weeping in remorse and desperation. And in *Aida* (1871), a father, Amonasro, uses paternal tenderness and nostalgia — as well as threats — to bend his daughter Aida to his will and betray her lover, Rhadames.

In Verdi, those fathers are powerful and ambivalent personalities. The tempestuous passions of fathers churn the cores of his operas as suffering sons and daughters sing "Padre, mio padre" in tenderness, or in terror, or in tears. Fathers and their conflict with their progeny intrigued Verdi to such an extent that throughout his life he would contemplate, but not bring to fruition, an opera based on one of the greatest and conflicted father figures: Shakespeare's *King Lear.*

As Violetta rises to the sacrifice, she asks Germont: "Embrace me like a daughter." But the essence of the drama, hers inner conflicts and fears of her destiny, are revealed as an aside to herself during her confrontation with Germont: "Così alla misera, ch'è un di caduta, di piu risorgere speranza è muta" ("Such is the misery of a fallen woman who cannot be reborn, and for whom all hope has ended!") Violetta cannot shake her curse: in her own mind she is a guilty sinner. Violetta knows she is *La Traviata,* "the fallen woman."

Violetta faces confusion: how will she separate from Alfredo? She reasons that her only alternative is to make Alfredo hate her, and she will achieve this by telling Alfredo that she has decided to return to her former courtesan life of luxury and pleasure.

It is a heartbreaking moment when Violetta writes her parting letter to Alfredo, underscored with short, lamenting phrases from the clarinet that serves to narrate her excruciating pain. When Alfredo suddenly returns, Violetta pours out her heart: "Love me Alfredo, love me as I love you." It is a painful and agonizing moment, made more poignant by its underscore of the passionate love theme music from the prelude. Her next meeting with Alfredo will be humiliating as Alfredo's passionate love for Violetta will turn so abruptly into denunciation and hate: at Flora's party, in Act II - Scene 2, Alfredo will vent the agony of his betrayal and vengeance, made all the more heart-wrenching because Violetta is duty-bound to secrecy.

In the final act, Violetta senses death: she has consoled herself by giving what little money she has left to the poor. She reads aloud Giorgio Germont's letter, a moment of spoken rather than sung words that is underscored by a solo violin playing Alfredo's love melody: "Di quel amore."

In his letter, Germont is contrite and admits that he now realizes that he has been the cause of so much of her anguish. He has seen his son disgrace her in public, and he has heard her say in forgiveness: "Alfredo, Alfredo, you don't know how much I love you!" Begging forgiveness is the underlying theme of *La Traviata,* and contrition applies to all of the characters in the story.

With Alfredo's arrival, Violetta's final wishes have been fulfilled, and together they dream of their love's renewal. The grandeur and nobility of *La Traviata* music and story is revealed most emphatically in its final moments: Violetta is eloquent and heroic when she gives Alfredo her picture and asks him to give it to his future wife: her music is serene, understanding and compassionate, yet Verdi's mighty punctuated chords in his orchestral accompaniment represent pounding heartbeats that betray Violetta's agony: it is music that earned Verdi the epithet that he can bring tears from a stone.

The role of Violetta is perhaps the most demanding in the operatic repertory, but a fine singing actress with perfect vocal and dramatic perception and perspective can make it a supreme career achievement. Essentially, with the exception of the earlier moments of Act II - Scene 2, Violetta never leaves the stage.

Verdi made Violetta's music diverse: her music itself represents a metaphor for her changing character and temperament. In Act I, Violetta is a coloratura soprano whose florid and ornamented music represent her abandonment to pleasure: in Act II, she is a lyric soprano, a transformed woman who is no longer the radiant courtesan of Parisian society, but rather, a gracious and modest woman struggling in her battle with the inevitability of her fate; and in Act II - Scene 2 and Act III, she is a "lirico spinto," her voice containing vigorous lyricism reflecting her battle against tragic forces of destiny.

The real crowning achievement for a Violetta-soprano is to bestow upon the role its full meaning and power by conceiving the virtuoso music with brilliance and security, and at the same time, portray the character with aristocratic sensibility.

The singing-actress must never exaggerate, but at the same time, she must emphasize expressive details: her expressions of passion or agony must never lose dignity or betray her profound sorrow; and in her centerpiece, "Sempre libera," she must display an élan in its attack, a sophisticated bravura that can make the pulse quicken, but never lose the mood of desperate gaiety of those condemned courtesans.

Violetta's second act must pace the tension to effectively provide dramatic truth and feeling; it must convey her frightful agitation and premonition of doom, if not evil; she must feel oppressed while her heart breaks; her eternal parting must contain a pathos that wrings the heart. In the end, her portrayal must be an outcry from a stricken spirit, and therefore the role must be portrayed with a sense of tragic dignity.

La Traviata is a poignant story in which profound dramatic truth lies in the fullness and depth of the human suffering it portrays, and in the self-sacrificing love of a truly noble personality. Verdi's dignified expression of genuine humanity, and his miraculous power to convey those sentiments in his music, confirms his supreme understanding of the human heart.

Dumas wrote his story *La Dame aux Camélias,* begging the world to pity a spurned lover. Verdi added nobility, heart, and soul to the infamous "Lady of the Camellias," and provided immortality to the "woman with a heart of gold."

In *La Traviata,* Verdi expressed his exalted vision of humanity and the human spirit: in his story, "the fallen woman" is redeemed through the nobility of her sacrifice.

His *La Traviata* story is not about the death of love, nor the death of lovers. His story is a thundering yet intimate declaration about the redemptive value of humanity's greatest aspiration: love.

La Traviata

Principal Characters in *La Traviata*
Brief StorySynopsis
Story Narrative with Music Highlight Examples

Principal Characters in La Traviata

Violetta Valery, a beautiful young Parisian courtesan	Soprano
Alfredo Germont, a young nobleman from Provence	Tenor
Giorgio Germont, Alfredo's father	Baritone
Flora Bervoix, a courtesan friend of Violetta	Mezzo-soprano
Baron Douphol, Violetta's friend and protector	Bass
Dr. Grenvil, Violetta's friend and her doctor	Bass
Marquis d'Obigny, Flora's friend	Bass
Gastone, a friend of Alfredo	Tenor
Annina, Violetta's maid	Mezzo-soprano
Giuseppe, Violetta's servant	Tenor

Ladies and gentlemen, friends, guests, and servants of Violetta and Flora, entertainers dressed as matadors, picadors, and gypsies.

TIME: 1850
PLACE: Paris and the countryside

Brief Story Synopsis

Violetta Valery, a courtesan, has become afflicted with consumption (tuberculosis). A young nobleman, Alfredo Germont, falls in love with her, and persuades her to abandon her profession and live with him in the countryside outside Paris.

Alfredo's father, Giorgio Germont, visits Violetta and demands that she must abandon her affair with his son because their relationship has created a scandal that has ruined his daughter's prospects for marriage. Violetta accedes to his demands and abandons Alfredo by telling him in a letter that she no longer loves him: she is returning to her former life as a courtesan.

Shortly thereafter, at a party, the spurned Alfredo rages at Violetta and publicly denounces her. Violetta is helpless and honor-bound by her promise to Alfredo's father, and cannot reveal that in truth, she sacrificed their love for his family's honor.

Violetta's illness becomes fatal. Alfredo returns to her after he learns that her betrayal was in truth a noble sacrifice. The lovers renew their intimacy and dream of a future together, but Violetta's illness overcomes her, and she dies.

Story Narrative with Music Highlight Examples

Prelude:

La Traviata's prelude presents two contrasting musical themes; both are musical portraits of the heroine, Violetta Valery. The first theme is extremely poignant, intended to convey the tragic heroine's suffering and despair. The theme reappears at the beginning of Act III, emphasizing the hopelessness of Violetta's illness.

Violetta's theme of despair:

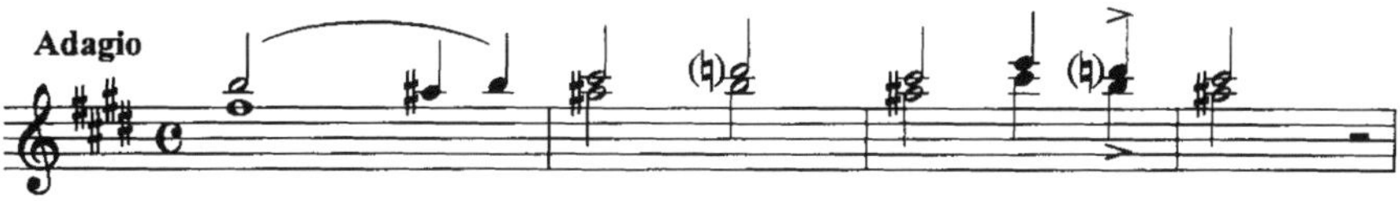

The second theme is the Love theme, the consuming passion of Alfredo and Violetta that reappears in Act II.

Love theme:

Act 1: The Drawing Room in Violetta's home in Paris.

Violetta and her courtesan friends host a sumptuous party. Alfredo Germont, a young nobleman from Provence who has been secretly admiring Violetta, is formally introduced to the beautiful hostess by his friend, Gastone. The guests and Violetta encourage Alfredo to improvise a toast celebrating the joys of wine, love, and carefree pleasure, leading to the exuberant Drinking Song: "Libiamo." During the interplay of words between Violetta and Alfredo, he suggests that their destiny is to fall in love with each other.

Drinking Song: "Libiamo, libiamo nei lieti calici"

The guests depart to an adjoining salon, but Violetta remains behind because she suddenly feels ill and faint. She is besieged by a racking cough, unaware that these symptoms are omens of fatal tuberculosis (consumption).

Of all of her guests, only Alfredo has remained behind. Alfredo suspects the depth of her illness and boldly blames it on the immoral and fatiguing life she leads. He then daringly proposes that if they were to fall in love, he would take care of her and nurture her back to health.

Impetuously, he pours out his love for Violetta, revealing that for over a year he has been tormented by his secret passion for her. Alfredo's aria, "Un di felice eterea" ("One happy, heavenly day, your image appeared before me"). Alfredo's passionate expression of love for Violetta climaxes with the words "Di quell'amor, quell'amor ch'è palpito" ("It is a love that throbs like the entire universe.")

"Di quell'amor, quell'amor ch'è palpito"

Violetta is surprised yet flattered by Alfredo's impassioned expressions of love for her. Even though deep sensibilities have been aroused in her, she frivolously pretends indifference and dismisses his passions: "I can only offer you friendship."

Violetta gives Alfredo a camellia and invites him to visit her again when the flower has faded. When he impetuously asks when that will be, she answers, "tomorrow." Alfredo ecstatically kisses her hand and leaves.

The guests make their farewells, and Violetta, now alone, admits to herself that she is truly moved by Alfredo's sincere affection and tender words of love. She admits to herself that she is experiencing sudden mysterious sensations, feelings that no man has ever awakened in her.

Violetta soliloquizes, "to love, or not to love." She confronts her inner contradictions and anxieties, and concludes that Alfredo's words of love are indeed foolish illusions: she is a sick woman, and her life has become an indulgence in the fleeting joys and worldly pleasures of courtesan life. Her life-style precludes real love: a love affair would only be nonsense and a folly; Violetta must always be free.

As Violetta addresses the conflict of her strange feelings, she comments, "È strano" ("I feel so strange"), and then she speculates, "Ah fors' è lui che l'anima" ("Perhaps he will rid me of my unhappiness, and bring joy to my tormented soul!")

"Ah fors'è lui che l'anima"

Violetta shakes off her fantasizing and reverses gear, rejecting the idea of love as "Follie" ("What nonsense! This folly is a mad illusion.") She proceeds to praise liberty, freedom, and pleasure in the dazzling coloratura aria "Sempre libera" ("I must always be free.")

But Violetta's protective armor has been pierced. Emotion has overpowered reason, and Violetta's praise of liberty becomes haunted by her imagination as she hears the echo of Alfredo's ecstatic love song, "Di quell'amor, quell'amore ch'è palpito." Nevertheless, Violetta reaffirms her rejection of love by vowing resolutely that she will always be free.

"Sempre libera"

Allegro brillante
VIOLETTA

Sempre li - be -ra deg - g' i - o fol - leg-gia-re di gioia in gio - ia,
I must always be free to enjoy the pleasures of life.

Act II - Scene 1: Violetta's country villa outside of Paris.

Five months have passed, and Alfredo and Violetta are now living an idyllic life together in her country villa far from the social whirl of Paris. Violetta, fully conquered by love, obeyed the call from her heart and abandoned her courtesan life.

Alfredo rejoices in the fulfillment and peace of their life together.

"De'miei bollenti spiriti"

Andante
ALFREDO

De' miei bol-len - ti spi - ri - ti
She has tempered my ardent passions.

Violetta has been paying for their country life of romantic bliss, but she is running out of money. Annina, Violetta's maid, tells Alfredo that to offset their mounting expenses, she had gone to Paris to arrange for the sale of some of Violetta's possessions. Alfredo is shocked and chagrined, his pride and honor tarnished. He decides to leave for Paris himself in order to personally raise money.

Violetta's new life has transformed her: she is no longer the radiant courtesan of Parisian society, but now a gracious and modest woman. The core and pivotal moment in the drama occurs with the arrival of Alfredo's father, Giorgio Germont.

Germont's musical entrance expresses a sense of coldness and hostility: Germont symbolizes morality, worldly and family values.

Germont's entrance:

Germont ceremoniously introduces himself and attacks at once: "You are looking at Alfredo's father," and he continues, "Yes, I am the father of that reckless young man who is rushing to ruin by his infatuation for you."

Germont has arrived to implore — and demand — that Violetta give up her scandalous liaison with his son, a relationship he conceives not only to be Alfredo's boyish entanglement, but one that is ruining their family's reputation. They confront each other in a series of duets, more aptly, a series of duels that are filled with Violetta's passionate lyric outbursts expressing shock, anguish, tears, and despair, but eventually, defeat and concession to his demands.

Germont tells Violetta, "But he wants to give you his fortune." Violetta maintains her dignity against his accusations and proudly advises Germont that she herself has sold most of her own possessions in order to maintain their life-style; in effect, she proves that she is not a kept woman, nor that she is dependent on his son's financial support. Germont controverts her defense and his momentary defeat by accusing Violetta of living on immoral earnings.

Germont pleads with Violetta to abandon Alfredo, explaining that the sacrifice he asks is not for Alfredo's sake alone, but for both his children; in particular, his "pure and angelic daughter." He explains that his daughter cannot marry until Alfredo — and his family — is freed from the disgrace of his scandalous liaison with Violetta.

"Pura siccome un angelo"

Violetta persuades Germont that she truly loves Alfredo; nevertheless, Germont is intransigent and will not ease up on his demand that they separate. Their conversation takes on a new dimension as Germont changes from the voice of morality to that of patronizing respect, sympathy, and understanding: his move from harshness to sympathy and understanding will become his ultimate weapon that he will use to persuade Violetta in order to gain his victory.

Violetta herself is shaken by his demands, and moves through an entire spectrum of profound and distraught feelings and emotions; nevertheless, she will slowly be forced from strength to defeat. Violetta imagines that to fulfill Germont's request, she must only part from Alfredo for a short time: until after his sister's marriage. But Germont insists that she must abandon Alfredo totally — and forever.

Violetta protests that she would rather die than leave Alfredo, explaining that she senses that she is mortally ill, that she has no friends or family, and that their love has become her only comfort and solace. Germont does not believe that Violetta is really ill. (In Dumas's original he says, "Let us be calm and not exaggerate. You mistake your illness for what is nothing more than the fatigue caused by your restless (courtesan) life.")

Germont is relentless. He tries to persuade Violetta to think of the future when she will no longer be young, and Alfredo, with male fickleness, will have allowed his affections to stray. He condemns their love as an unholy affair that has not been blessed by the church, and therefore, there is nothing sacred to hold them together for a lifetime.

Violetta senses defeat, and reflects on the hopelessness of her position. She senses that she has no alternative and reluctantly decides to yield to Germont: Violetta agrees to abandon Alfredo; her ultimate reasoning is that if she harmed Alfredo's future, her soul would be damned and condemned.

Violetta asks Germont to tell Alfredo's sister that, for her sake, an unfortunate woman is sacrificing her only dream of happiness: the joy she had finally found through her love for Alfredo.

"Dite alla giovane, si bella e pura"

Germont praises Violetta's generosity, and tells her to be courageous; her noble sacrifice will bring its own just and heavenly reward. Violetta makes a last request, that only after she is dead shall Germont tell Alfredo that she loved him so profoundly that she would sacrifice her own happiness for his sake. Germont departs, assuring Violetta again that "Heaven will reward her" for her noble deed.

Violetta, now alone, writes a farewell letter to Alfredo. In order to make her parting believable to Alfredo, she concludes that she must make him hate her: she explains to Alfredo in her letter that the call of her former life is too strong to resist, and therefore, she has decided to leave him and return to Paris.

While Violetta is writing, Alfredo suddenly appears: both are overcome with a strange sense of tension and uneasiness. Agonizingly, Violetta embraces Alfredo, and then bursts into a passionate declaration of her love for him; the underlying music is the theme heard earlier in the Prelude identifying their love for each other. Violetta then abruptly tears herself from Alfredo, and rushes out, her "addio" intended to be a final farewell.

"Amami Alfredo"

Giuseppe, a servant, advises the bewildered and perplexed Alfredo that Violetta has left for Paris. Alfredo assumes that she has gone to sell more of her possessions. But a messenger suddenly arrives to deliver Violetta's farewell letter. Alfredo reads the letter, and becomes devastated: Violetta has betrayed him.

Anticipating Violetta's actions and his son's remorse, Giorgio Germont had been waiting patiently in the outside garden, fulfilling his promise to Violetta to provide consolation to his son. Alfredo is distraught by Violetta's abandonment of him, but his father, aware of her motives, is duty bound to conceal the truth from his son. Germont tries to persuade Alfredo that his loss of Violetta will ultimately be for his own good, and then, evoking Provence, appeals to him to return to the serenity of home and family.

"Di Provenza il mar il sol che dal cor il cancelò?"

Nevertheless, Germont's consolation to his son is in vain. Alfredo has seen Flora's invitation, feels betrayed, and rages in anger and jealousy; he rushes off for revenge on the woman who has abandoned him. He will go to Flora's party and confront Violetta.

Act II - Scene 2: Flora's Villa.

At a masked ball at Violetta's friend Flora's villa, fortune-telling gypsies read palms, and dancers, dressed as matadors and picadors, entertain the guests.

A bitter Alfredo joins the party and sits down to play at the gaming tables. Violetta enters on the arm of Baron Douphol, her friend and "protector." Douphol joins the card game and Alfredo wins every hand, claiming sarcastically that he is "lucky at cards but unlucky in love."

Alfredo's sarcastic comments to his rival Baron Douphol, and his continuing luck in winning, provoke Douphol's resentment. Insults follow, but their quarrel is temporarily avoided as the company departs to an adjoining room for dinner.

Violetta leaves the dinner in agitation and alarm and sends for Alfredo to warn him that Baron Douphol is resolved to challenge him to a duel. Violetta fears for Alfredo's life, and urges him to leave, but Alfredo, in his jealous rage, accuses Violetta of being more afraid that she might lose Douphol, her "protector."

Alfredo affirms that he will only leave if Violetta joins him, but Violetta cannot leave with Alfredo: in effect, reuniting with Alfredo would violate her sacred promise to Giorgio Germont. With supreme effort to dissuade Alfredo, Violetta lies, telling Alfredo that she cannot leave with him because she indeed now loves Baron Douphol.

Alfredo erupts in jealousy and rage. He summons all the guests, and before the entire assemblage, denounces and insults Violetta, admitting his own shame at having allowed a woman to squander her fortune on him.

Alfredo hurls a purse containing his winnings at Violetta: he wants all to witness that he has repaid her in full for her favors. The entire gathering becomes shocked and outraged, and responds to his outburst with indignation.

Suddenly, Giorgio Germont appears. He has overheard Alfredo's contemptible insults at Violetta, and humiliated by his son's wayward behavior, severely reproaches him.

Alfredo awakens to his foolishness, and becomes overcome with remorse and shame. Violetta, restrained by her promise to Alfredo's father, regrets that she cannot reveal the truth to Alfredo and express her true and heartfelt love for him. In a majestic and powerful ensemble with heartrending music of sublime, heroic proportions, Violetta prays that one day Alfredo will know the truth of her sacrifice. As the scene concludes, Violetta faints, and Baron Douphol, breathing fury and revenge, challenges Alfredo to a duel.

"Alfredo, Alfredo"

Act III: One month later. Violetta's bedroom.

The entire mood of the final act of *La Traviata* conveys a deep sense of desolation, despair, and pity. Violetta's illness, her suffering and pain, have now become more intense and recovery is beyond hope: the beautiful courtesan has now become a mere shadow of her former self and senses that she is close to death. Dr. Grenvil tries to instill hope and courage in his friend and patient, but in an aside to the maid Annina, he confesses that all hope is futile and the end is near.

Violetta reads a letter from Giorgio Germont which thanks her for having kept her promise. She also learns that the duel had taken place, that Alfredo was unharmed, and that Baron Douphol was only slightly wounded. Germont confesses that he has told Alfredo the truth about Violetta's profound and selfless sacrifice, and that Alfredo is en route to see her to beg her forgiveness for his rashness.

With touching nostalgia, Violetta yearns for a reunion with Alfredo, and reminisces about the happy months they spent together. Violetta prays to God to pardon and have pity on the "traviata," the "fallen woman." (The only time "traviata" is mentioned in the opera.)

"Addio del passato"

Alfredo arrives and the reunited lovers exchange ecstatic and rapturous sentiments of love and forgiveness. They reminisce about their past happiness, and in the duet "Parigi o caro" ("Dear Paris"), they dream of leaving Paris for a new and radiant future together.

Violetta's strength begins to fail rapidly, and she appeals to God not to let her die so young: now that Alfredo has returned, she has been rejuvenated and wants to live.

Giorgio Germont arrives and struck with remorse and guilt, penitently admits that he had been the cause of so much of Violetta's sorrow, and fulfilling his promise, embraces her as if she were his own daughter.

Violetta, in a noble gesture, gives Alfredo a medallion containing her portrait.She tells him that if he marries in the future, he is to give it to his wife as assurance that Violetta is in Heaven and praying for them.

"Prendi quest'è l'imagine"

Violetta feels a strange and mysterious sense of new strength, a momentary resurgence of life. In one last gesture, she tries to hold on to Alfredo and to life, but suddenly, the last breath leaves Violetta.

"La Traviata," the "fallen women," has died.

Libretto

Act I

Prelude

Violetta's theme of despair:

Love theme:

The banquet hall of Violetta Valery's elegant home in Paris. Violetta is in conversation with Doctor Grenvil and several friends. Other guests arrive, among them Baron Douphol. Violetta's friend, Flora, arrives on the arm of the Marquis d'Obigny.

CORO I:
Dell'invito trascorsa è già l'ora.
Voi tardaste.

CHORUS I:
You've arrived much later than expected.

CORO II:
Giocammo da Flora. E giocando
quell'ore volar.

CHORUS 2:
We were at Flora's playing cards, and the time seemed to fly by.

VIOLETTA:
Flora, amici, la notte che resta
d'altre gioie qui fate brillar.
Fra le tazze è più viva la festa.

VIOLETTA:
Flora, my friends, let's enjoy the rest of the evening. Have a drink and the party will be livelier.

FLORA E MARCHESE:
E goder voi potrete?

FLORA and MARQUIS:
Will you join the fun?

VIOLETTA:
Lo voglio; al piacere m'affido, ed io
soglio col tal farmaco i mali sopir.

VIOLETTA:
Of course I will: a good time always cures my pains.

TUTTI:
Sì, la vita s'addoppia al gioir.

ALL:
Yes, joy makes us live longer!

The Viscount arrives, then Gastone with his friend, Alfredo Germont.

GASTONE:
In Alfredo Germont, o signora, ecco un altro che molto vi onora; pochi amici a lui simili sono.

GASTONE: *(introducing Alfredo)*
My dear lady, you will find yet another admirer in Alfredo Germont. I assure you that there are few friends like him.

VIOLETTA:
Mio Visconte, mercè di tal dono.

VIOLETTA:
Viscount, thank you for the privilege.

Violetta extends her hand to Alfredo, who kisses it politely.

MARCHESE:
Caro Alfredo

MARQUIS:
My dear Alfredo!

ALFREDO:
Marchese!

ALFREDO:
Why, it's the Marquis!
(They shake hands)

GASTONE:
T'ho detto: l'amistà qui s'intreccia al diletto.

GASTONE: *(aside to Alfredo)*
Didn't I tell you that pleasure and friendship go together here.

VIOLETTA:
Pronto è il tutto?

Miei cari sedete: È al convito che s'apre ogni cor.

VIOLETTA: *(to the servants)*
Is everything ready?
(a servant nods)
My friends, be seated and enjoy the banquet wholeheartedly.

TUTTI:
Ben diceste le cure segrete. Fuga sempre l'amico licor.

ALL:
It is true that all troubles vanish with wine.

The guests assume their places at the dinner table. Violetta sits between Alfredo and Gastone. While the guests are being served, Violetta and Gastone converse in a whisper.

GASTONE:
Sempre Alfredo a voi pensa.

GASTONE: *(to Violetta)*
Alfredo is always thinking about you.

VIOLETTA:
Scherzate?

VIOLETTA:
Are you joking?

GASTONE:
Egra foste, e ogni dì con affanno qui volo di voi chiese.

GASTONE:
During your illness he came here every day to ask how you were.

VIOLETTA:
Cessate. Nulla son io per lui!

VIOLETTA:
Come now! I don't mean anything to him!

GASTONE:
Non v'inganno.

GASTONE:
I'm serious.

VIOLETTA:
Vero è dunque? Onde è ciò?
Nol comprendo.

VIOLETTA: *(to Alfredo)*
Is it really true? Is it so?
I don't understand.

ALFREDO:
Si, egli è ver.

ALFREDO: *(sighing)*
Yes, it's true.

VIOLETTA:
Le mie grazie vi rendo.

Voi Barone, feste altrettanto

VIOLETTA:
Then I am indeed grateful.
(turning to the Baron)
You, Baron, were not so attentive.

BARONE:
Vi conosco da un anno soltanto.

BARON:
But I only know you for a year.

VIOLETTA:
Ed ei solo da qualche minuto.

VIOLETTA:
And he only knows me for barely a minute.

FLORA:
Meglio fora se aveste taciuto.

FLORA: *(aside to the Baron.)*
It would have been better if you had kept quiet.

BARONE:
Mi è increscioso quel giovin.

BARON: *(to Flora, indicating Alfredo)*
That young man really annoys me.

FLORA: Perchè? A me invece simpatico egli è.	**FLORA:** Why? I find him quite charming.
GASTONE: E tu dunque non apri più bocca?	**GASTONE:** *(to Alfredo)* You have nothing else to say?
MARCHESE: È a madama che scuoterlo tocca.	**MARQUIS:** *(to Violetta)* You will have to inspire him.
VIOLETTA: Sarò l'Ebe che versa.	**VIOLETTA:** I'll be Hebe and pour the wine for you. *(Violetta pours wine for Alfredo.)*
ALFREDO: E ch'io bramo immortal come quella.	**ALFREDO:** *(gallantly)* And like her I'll immortalize you.
TUTTI: Beviamo!	**ALL:** Let's drink!
GASTONE: O barone, nè un verso, nè un viva troverete in quest'ora giuliva?	**GASTONE:** Baron, do you have a verse or a toast to enliven this festive hour?

The Baron nods negatively. Gastone turns to Alfredo.

Dunque a te.	Then it's up to you.
TUTTI: Sì, sì, un brindisi.	**ALL:** Yes, let's have a toast!
ALFREDO: L'estro non m'arride.	**ALFREDO:** I'm not inspired yet.
GASTONE: E non sei tu maestro?	**GASTONE:** Aren't you a master at it?
ALFREDO: Vi fia grato?	**ALFREDO:** *(to Violetta)* Would you like me to?
VIOLETTA: Sì.	**VIOLETTA:** Yes.
ALFREDO: Sì? L'ho già in cor.	**ALFREDO:** Yes? Then I'll be delighted.

MARCHESE:
Dunque attenti!

MARQUIS:
Attention everybody!

TUTTI:
Sì, attenti al cantor!

ALL:
Yes, listen to the toast!

ALFREDO:
Libiamo nei lieti calici che la bellezza infiora, e la fuggevol ora s'inebri a voluttà.

Libiamo nei dolci fremiti che suscita l'amore, poiché quell'occhio al core ogni potente va.

Libiamo, amor fra i calici più caldi baci avrà.

ALFREDO:
Let's drink from theses cups adorned with flowers, to the fleeting hours of pleasure.

Let's drink to love's gentle throbbing, that pierces the heart with all its power.

Let's drink to love's warm kisses flowing from these cups.

TUTTI:
Libiamo, amor fra i calici più caldi baci avrà.

ALL:
Let's drink to love's warm kisses flowing from these cups.

VIOLETTA:
Tra voi saprò dividere il tempo mio giocondo; tutto è follia nel mondo ciò che non è piacer.

Godiam, fugace e rapido è il gaudio dell'amore; è un fior che nasce e muore, nè più si può goder.
Godiam c'invita un fervido accento lusinghier.

VIOLETTA:
I spend my time happily amongst you. Everything in the world is folly if one cannot enjoy pleasure.

Let's enjoy pleasure, for the joys of love fade quickly, like a flower that is born and dies.
Let's enjoy pleasure, while its passion and temptation invite us.

TUTTI:
Godiam la tazza e il cantico la notte abbella e il riso; in questo paradiso ne scopra il nuovo dì.

ALL:
Let's enjoy drinking and singing which enhance the night with laughter. May dawn never arrive in this paradise.

VIOLETTA:
La vita è nel tripudio.

VIOLETTA: *(to Alfredo)*
Life is full of pleasure.

ALFREDO:
Quando non s'ami ancora.

ALFREDO: *(to Violetta.)*
Until one discovers love.

VIOLETTA:
Nol dite a chi l'ignora.

VIOLETTA: *(to Alfredo)*
That's something I haven't discovered yet.

ALFREDO:
È il mio destin così.

ALFREDO: *(to Violetta.)*
Well then that's my destiny.

TUTTI:
Godiam la tazza e il cantico la notte abbella e il riso; in questo paradiso ne scopra il nuovo dì.

ALL:
Let's enjoy drinking and singing which enhance the night with laughter. May dawn never arrive in this paradise.

(Music is heard from the drawing room)

Che è ciò?

What is that?

VIOLETTA:
Non gradireste ora le danze?

VIOLETTA:
Wouldn't you like to dance now?

TUTTI:
Oh, il gentil pensier! Tutti accettiamo!

ALL:
How gracious of you! We'd love to!

VIOLETTA:
Usciamo dunque!

VIOLETTA:
Let's go then!

Violetta suddenly has a coughing spell; she falters and turns pale.

VIOLETTA:
È colta da subito pallore. Ohimè!

VIOLETTA:
All of a sudden I don't feel well!

TUTTI:
Che avete?

ALL:
What's the matter?

VIOLETTA: Nulla, nulla!	**VIOLETTA:** It's nothing, nothing!
TUTTI: Che mai v'arresta?	**ALL:** Then why do you stay behind?
VIOLETTA: Usciamo!	**VIOLETTA:** Let's go on!
O Dio!	*(Violetta sinks into a chair)* Oh, God!
TUTTI: Ancora!	**ALL:** Again!
ALFREDO: Voi soffrite?	**ALFREDO:** Are you in pain?
TUTTI: O ciel! Ch'è questo?	**ALL:** Oh heavens! What can it be?
VIOLETTA: Un tremito che provo or là passate.	**VIOLETTA:** I felt a sudden chill but it passed. *(Motions all to go to the drawing room)*
Tra poco anch'io sarò.	I'll join you in a minute.
TUTTI: Come bramate.	**ALL:** As you wish.
	(All enter the drawing room except Alfredo)
VIOLETTA: O qual pallor!	**VIOLETTA:** *(looking into a mirror)* Goodness, how pale I am! *(She turns and sees Alfredo)*
Voi qui!	You're still here?
ALFREDO: Cessata è l'ansia che vi turbò?	**ALFREDO:** Are you feeling better?
VIOLETTA: Sto meglio.	**VIOLETTA:** Yes, I'm better.

ALFREDO:
Ah, in cotal guisa v'ucciderete aver v'è d'uopo cura dell'esser vostro.

ALFREDO:
This life-style will kill you. You must take better care of yourself.

VIOLETTA:
E lo potrei?

VIOLETTA:
You think I could?

ALFREDO:
Se mia foste, custode io veglierei pe' vostri soavi dì.

ALFREDO:
If you were mine, I would take care of you day and night.

VIOLETTA:
Che dite?
Ha forse alcuno cura di me?

VIOLETTA:
What are you saying?
Does someone really care for me?

ALFREDO:
Perchè nessuno al mondo v'ama.

ALFREDO: *(impetuously)*
No one in the world loves you.

VIOLETTA:
Nessun?

VIOLETTA:
No one?

ALFREDO:
Tranne sol io!

ALFREDO:
No one except me!

VIOLETTA::
Gli è vero! Sì grande amor dimenticato avea.

VIOLETTA: *(laughing)*
Really! I had forgotten about your great love for me!

ALFREDO:
Ridete? E in voi v'ha un core?

ALFREDO:
Are you mocking me? Have you no heart?

VIOLETTA:
Un cor? Sì forse e a che lo richiedete?

VIOLETTA:
A heart? Perhaps, but why do you ask?

ALFREDO:
O, se ciò fosse, non potreste allora celiar.

ALFREDO:
Oh, because if you had a heart, you would not joke about this.

VIOLETTA:
Dite davvero?

VIOLETTA:
Are you serious?

ALFREDO:
Io non v'inganno.

ALFREDO:
I wouldn't deceive you.

VIOLETTA:
Da molto è che mi amate?

VIOLETTA:
Have you loved me for a long time?

ALFREDO:
Ah sì, da un anno.
Un dì, felice, eterea, mi balenaste innante,
e da quel dì tremante vissi d'ignoto amor.

ALFREDO:
Yes, for a year.
One happy, heavenly day, your image appeared before me,
and since that trembling moment, I have secretly loved you.

Di quell'amor ch'è palpito dell'universo intero, misterioso, altero, croce e delizia al cor.

It is a love that throbs like the entire universe, bringing mysterious pain and ecstasy to my heart.

VIOLETTA:
Ah, se ciò è ver, fuggitemi solo amistade io v'offro: amar non so, nè soffro un così eroico amor.
Io sono franca, ingenua; altra cercar dovete; non arduo troverete dimenticarmi allor.

VIOLETTA:
If that's true, then leave me, for I can only offer you friendship! I don't know love, nor want to suffer in heroic amours.
I must tell you frankly and genuinely, that you won't receive arduous love from me. So find another and forget me.

GASTONE:
Ebben! Che diavol fate?

GASTONE: *(joining them)*
Well! What are you up to?

VIOLETTA:
Si foleggiava.

VIOLETTA:
Just talking nonsense.

GASTONE:
Ah! Ah! Sta ben, restate.

GASTONE:
So! Very well then, go on.

VIOLETTA:
Amor dunque non più. Vi garba il patto?

VIOLETTA: *(to Alfredo)*
No more talk of love then. Agreed?

ALFREDO:
Io v'obbedisco. Parto.

ALFREDO:
I'll do whatever you say. I'm leaving.

VIOLETTA: A tal giungeste?	**VIOLETTA:** You're leaving already?
	(giving him a flower from her corsage)
Prendete questo fiore.	Here, take this flower.
ALFREDO: Perchè?	**ALFREDO:** Why?
VIOLETTA: Per riportarlo.	**VIOLETTA:** To bring it back to me.
ALFREDO: Quando?	**ALFREDO:** When?
VIOLETTA: Quando sarà appassito.	**VIOLETTA:** When it has faded.
ALFREDO: O ciel! Domani.	**ALFREDO:** Tomorrow then?
VIOLETTA: Ebben, domani.	**VIOLETTA:** Very well, tomorrow.
ALFREDO: Io son felice!	**ALFREDO:***(excitedly)* I'm so happy!
VIOLETTA:: D'amarmi dite ancora?	**VIOLETTA:** And do you still say you love me?
ALFREDO: Oh, quanto v'amo!	**ALFREDO:** Oh, I adore you immensely!
VIOLETTA: Partite?	**VIOLETTA:** You're leaving?
ALFREDO: Parto.	**ALFREDO:** Yes I am.
	(Alfredo kisses her hand)
VIOLETTA:: Addio.	**VIOLETTA:** Goodbye.

ALFREDO:
Di più non bramo?

ALFREDO:
Could I want anything more?
(Alfredo departs)

The party guests return from the ballroom.

TUTTI:
Si ridesta in ciel l'aurora, e n'è forza di partir.
Mercè a voi, gentil signora, di sì splendido gioir.
La città di feste è piena, volge il tempo dei piacer.
Nel riposo ancor la lena si ritempri per goder,

ALL:
Dawn is breaking, telling us that we must leave now.
Thank you, genteel lady, for the wonderful enjoyment this evening.
In the city, the sounds of laughter fill the silence of the night.
But we must rest so that we can again enjoy life's pleasures.
(All the guests depart)

VIOLETTA::
È strano! È strano! In core scolpiti ho quegli accenti! Sarìa per me sventura un serio amore? Che risolvi, o turbata anima mia?

Null'uomo ancora t'accendeva.
O gioia ch'io non conobbi, essere amata amando! E sdegnarla poss'io per l'aride follie del viver mio?

VIOLETTA: *(alone)*
I feel so strange! I feel so strange! His words are carved in my heart. Would a serious love be fatal to me? What is the solution for my troubled soul?

No man has yet stirred love in me. Oh, I've never known such joy, to be loved and loving! Should I reject it now for all the empty follies in my life?

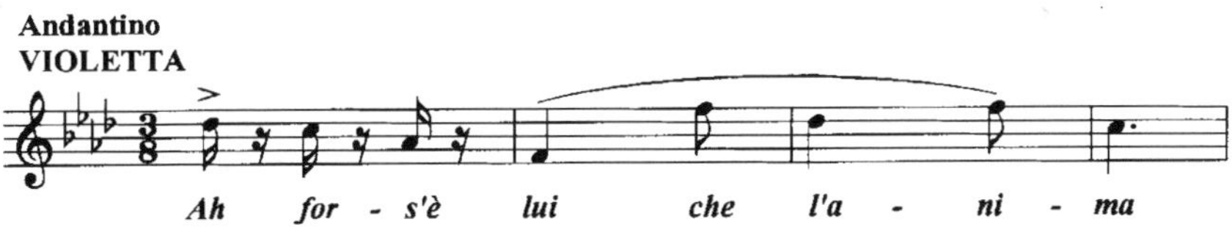

Ah, fors'è lui che l'anima solinga nè tumulti godea sovente pingere de' suoi colori occulti!

Lui che modesto e vigile all'egre soglie ascese, e nuova febbre accese, destandomi all'amor.
A quell'amor ch'è palpito dell'universo intero, misterioso, altero, croce e delizia al cor.

Perhaps he will rid me of my unhappiness, and bring joy to my tormented soul!

He is modest, forthright and honorable, and has stirred my emotions by awakening love.
It is a love that throbs like the entire universe, bringing mysterious pain and ecstasy to my heart.

A me fanciulla, un candido e trepido desire questi effigiò dolcissimo Signor dell'avvenire. Quando nè cieli il raggio di sua beltè vedea. E tutta me pascea di quel divino error. Sentì a che amore è palpito dell'universo intero, misterioso, altero, croce e delizia al cor!

When I was a child, I had gentle visions of the man in my future: so handsome and divine.
I felt love throbbing like the entire universe, bringing mysterious pain and ecstasy to my heart!

After a moment of rapt concentration, Violetta suddenly cries out.

Follie! Follie delirio vano è questo! Povera donna, sola abbandonata in questo popoloso deserto che appellano Parigi. Che spero or più?
Che far degg'io?
Gioire, di voluttà nei vortici perire.

What nonsense! This folly is a mad illusion! I'm an unfortunate, lonely woman, abandoned in this populous desert called Paris. What more can I hope for? What must I do?
Just seek pleasure and perish in this turmoil.

Sempre libera degg'io folleggiar di gioia in gioia. Vo' che scorra il viver mio pei sentieri del piacer. Nasca il giorno, o il giorno muoia, sempre lieta ne' ritrovi a diletti sempre nuovi dee volare il mio pensier.

I must always be free to enjoy the pleasures of life. I want to glide through life on the path of pleasure. Whether day or night, I yearn for happiness and new joys, always flying on the wings of desire.

End of Act I

Act II - Scene 1

Some months later.
A country villa on the outskirts of Paris.

ALFREDO:
Lunge da lei per me non v'ha diletto! Volaron già tre lune dacché la mia Violetta agi per me lasciò, dovizie, onori, e le pompose feste ove, agli omaggi avvezza, vedea schiavo ciascun di sua bellezza.
Ed or contenta in questi ameni luoghi tutto scorda per me. Qui presso a lei io rinascer mi sento, e dal soffio d'amor rigenerato scordo nè gaudii suoi tutto il passato.

ALFREDO:
I am unhappy away from her! Three months have now passed since my beloved Violetta gave up that luxury and glitter that she was accustomed to, as well as the gay festivities where men were captives of her beauty.
Yet, she is content in this idyllic place living only for me. Here, by her side, I feel myself reborn, rejuvenated by love, and forgetting the indulgences of the past.

Dè miei bollenti spiriti. Il giovanile ardore. Ella temprò col placido sorriso dell'amore! Dal dì che disse: vivere io voglio a te fedel. Dell'universo immemore io vivo quasi in ciel.

She has tempered my ardent passions with her smile, devotion, and love! Since she first said, "I want to live for your love," I feel like I am in heaven.

(The maid Annina enters)

ALFREDO:
Annina, donde vieni?

ALFREDO:
Annina! Where have you been?

ANNINA:
Da Parigi.

ANNINA:
To Paris.

ALFREDO:
Chi tel commise?

ALFREDO:
Who sent you there?

ANNINA:
Fu la mia signora.

ANNINA:
My mistress.

ALFREDO:
Perchè?

ALFREDO:
But why?

ANNINA:
Per alienar cavalli, cocchi, e quanto ancor possiede.

ANNINA:
To sell her horses, carriages, and other possessions.

ALFREDO:
Che mai sento!

ALFREDO:
What are you saying?

ANNINA:
Lo spendio è grande a viver qui solinghi.

ANNINA:
It's expensive to live here by yourselves.

ALFREDO:
E tacevi?

ALFREDO:
Why didn't you tell me?

ANNINA:
Mi fu il silenzio imposto.

ANNINA:
I was warned not to say anything.

ALFREDO:
Imposto! Or v'abbisogna?

ALFREDO:
Warned! How much money is needed?

ANNINA:
Mille luigi.

ANNINA:
A thousand louis.

ALFREDO:
Or vanne andrò a Parigi. Questo colloquio ignori la signora. Il tutto valgo a riparare ancora.

ALFREDO:
Go now! I will go to Paris, but not a word of this to your mistress. I still may be able to straighten everything out.

Annina departs, leaving Alfredo alone.

O mio rimorso! O infamia e vissi in tale errore? Ma il turpe sogno a frangere il ver mi balenò. Per poco in seno acquetati, o grido dell'onore; m'avrai securo vindice; quest'onta laverò.

Oh what remorse! Oh what shame from my mistakes! Truth has crushed the dream. I must quickly wash away this shame and restore my honor!

After Alfredo exits, Violetta appears.
She is followed by Annina, and then Giuseppe.

VIOLETTA: Alfredo!	**VIOLETTA:** Alfredo!
ANNINA: Per Parigi or partiva.	**ANNINA:** He has just left for Paris.
VIOLETTA: E tornerà?	**VIOLETTA:** And when is he coming back?
ANNINA: Pria che tramonti il giorno dirvel m'impose.	**ANNINA:** He said to tell you before sunset.
VIOLETTA: È strano!	**VIOLETTA:** That's strange!
GIUSEPPE: Per voi.	**GIUSEPPE:** *(handing Violetta a letter)* This is for you.
VIOLETTA:: Sta bene. In breve giungerà un uom d'affari. Entri all'istante.	**VIOLETTA:** Thanks. Soon a man will arrive to discuss a business matter. Show him in at once. *(Annina and Giuseppe exit)*
VIOLETTA: Ah, ah, scopriva Flora il mio ritiro! E m'invita a danzar per questa sera! Invan m'aspetterà.	**VIOLETTA:** *(reading the letter)* Ah, ah! So Flora has found me, and invites me to a ball tonight! I won't go; I'm no longer part of that life.

Violetta places Flora's invitation on a table.

GIUSEPPE: È qui un signore.	**GIUSEPPE:** A gentleman is here to see you.
VIOLETTA:: Ah! sarà lui che attendo.	**VIOLETTA:** Ah, he must be the man I'm expecting.

GERMONT: Madamigella Valery?	**GERMONT:** Mademoiselle Valery?

VIOLETTA:: Son io.	**VIOLETTA:** That is me.
GERMONT: D'Alfredo il padre in me vedete!	**GERMONT:** You are looking at Alfredo's father.
VIOLETTA: Voi!	**VIOLETTA:** *(surprised)* You!
GERMONT: Sì, dell'incauto, che a ruina corre, ammaliato da voi.	**GERMONT:** Yes, I am the father of that reckless young man who is rushing to ruin by his infatuation for you.
VIOLETTA:: Donna son io, signore, ed in mia casa; ch'io vi lasci assentite.Più per voi che per me.	**VIOLETTA:** *(affronted and resentful)* Sir, I am a lady, and I think it would be advisable for you to leave my house.
GERMONT: (Quai modi!) Pure...	**GERMONT:** (What gentility!) But...
VIOLETTA: Tratto in error voi foste.	**VIOLETTA:** You are making a false presumption.
GERMONT: Dè suoi beni dono vuol farvi.	**GERMONT:** But he wants to give you his fortune.
VIOLETTA: Non l'osò finora rifiuterei.	**VIOLETTA:** He has not dared. I would refuse it!
GERMONT: Pur tanto lusso?	**GERMONT:** Yet all this luxury?
VIOLETTA: A tutti è mistero quest'atto a voi nol sia.	**VIOLETTA:** Everyone wonders and is puzzled by it.

Violetta hands him some papers.

GERMONT: Ciel! Che discopro! D'ogni vostro avere or volete spogliarvi? Ah, il passato perchè, perchè v'accusa?	**GERMONT:** *(after examining them)* Heavens! What a revelation! You intend to sell all your possessions? Ah, but why? Does your past haunt you?

VIOLETTA:
Più non esiste or amo Alfredo, e Dio lo cancellò col pentimento mio.

VIOLETTA:
Since I love Alfredo, the past no longer exists. God has forgiven me.

GERMONT:
Nobili sensi invero!

GERMONT:
Noble sentiments indeed!

VIOLETTA:
O, come dolce mi suona il vostro accento!

VIOLETTA:
Oh, how soothing your words sound to me!

GERMONT:
Ed a tai sensi un sacrificio chieggo

GERMONT:
But from those sentiments I ask a sacrifice.

VIOLETTA:
Ah no, tacete. Terribil cosa chiedereste certo il previdi v'attesi era felice troppo.

VIOLETTA:
Ah no, don't say it! You'll surely ask something dreadful of me. I knew it, I was too happy.

GERMONT:
D'Alfredo il padre la sorte, l'avvenir domanda or qui de' suoi due figli.

GERMONT:
Fate demands that Alfredo's father pleads for the future of his two children.

VIOLETTA::
Di due figli?

VIOLETTA:
Two children?

GERMONT:
Sì. Pura siccome un angelo Iddio mi diè una figlia; se Alfredo nega riedere in seno alla famiglia, l'amato e amante giovane, cui sposa andar dovea, or si ricusa al vincolo che lieti ne rendea. Deh, non mutate in triboli le rose dell'amor ai preghi miei resistere non voglia il vostro cor.

GERMONT:
God gave me a daughter, who is pure as an angel. If Alfredo does not give up this sinful life and return to his family, my daughter's fiance will refuse to marry her.
Don't upset their future.
Don't resist me, follow your heart, and heed a father's prayers.

VIOLETTA::
Ah, comprendo, dovrò per alcun tempo da Alfredo allontanarmi doloroso fora per me pur.

VIOLETTA:
Ah, I understand. I must leave Alfredo for a short time, as painful as that will be for me.

GERMONT:
Non è ciò che chiedo.

GERMONT:
That's not all that I ask.

VIOLETTA:
Cielo, che più cercate?
Offersi assai!

VIOLETTA:
Heaven, what more then?
I have already offered so much!

GERMONT:
Pur non basta.

GERMONT:
It is not enough.

VIOLETTA:
Volete che per sempre a lui rinunzi?

VIOLETTA:
You want me to give him up forever?

GERMONT:
È d'uopo!

GERMONT:
That's how it has to be!

VIOLETTA:
Ah, no giammai! Non sapete quale affetto vivo, immenso m'arda in petto? Che nè amici, nè parenti Io non conto tra i viventi? E che Alfredo m'ha giurato che in lui tutto io troverò?

Non sapete che colpita d'altro morbo è la mia vita? Che già presso il fin ne vedo? Ch'io mi separi da Alfredo?
Ah, il supplizio è si spietato, che morir preferirò.

VIOLETTA:
Ah, no, never! Do you know the immense love that consumes me? That I have no friends, no relatives, and no one left in the world? And that Alfredo swore that he would be everything to me?

Do you know how terribly sick I am? That the end is near? And you want to separate me from Alfredo?
Ah, death would be less cruel than to give up Alfredo.

GERMONT:
È grave il sacrifizio. Ma pur tranquilla udite. Bella voi siete e giovane col tempo...

GERMONT:
It is a great sacrifice, but listen calmly. You are still young and beautiful, and with time...

VIOLETTA:
Ah, più non dite v'intendo m'è impossibile lui solo amar vogl'io.

VIOLETTA:
Please, say no more! It's impossible for me because I love him too much.

GERMONT:
Sia pure ma volubile sovente è l'uom.

GERMONT:
But remember that man is fickle.

VIOLETTA::
Gran Dio!

VIOLETTA: *(reacting in shock)*
Dear Heaven!

GERMONT:
Un dì, quando le veneri il tempo avrà fugate, fia presto il tedio a sorgere che sarà allor? Pensate. Per voi non avran balsamo i più soavi affetti poiché dal ciel non furono tai nodi benedetti.

GERMONT:
Some day, when his passions have faded, and weariness and boredom sets in, then what? Think about it. Remember that your relationship has not been blessed by Heaven.

VIOLETTA:
È vero!

VIOLETTA:
That's true!

GERMONT:
Ah, dunque sperdasi tal sogno seduttore siate di mia famiglia l'angiol consolatore. Deh, pensateci, ne siete in tempo ancor. è Dio che ispira, o giovine tai detti a un genitor.

GERMONT:
Ah, therefore forget your brazen dreams and be a consoling angel to my loved ones. Think Violetta, that it is God who inspires you to heed the words of a father.

VIOLETTA:
(Così alla misera ch'è un dì caduta, di più risorgere speranza è muta! Se pur beneficio le indulga Iddio, l'uomo implacabile per lei sarà.)

VIOLETTA: *(sorrowfully)*
(Such is the misfortune of a fallen woman who cannot be reborn, and for whom all hope has ended! God is merciful but society condemns her forever.)

Dite alla giovine. sì bella e pura, ch'avvi una vittima della sventura, cui resta un unico raggio di bene, che a lei il sacrifica e che morrà!

Tell the young woman, so beautiful and pure, that an unfortunate woman, crushed by despair, makes a sacrifice for her to be happy, and then will die!

GERMONT:
Sì, piangi, o misera, supremo il veggo. È il sacrificio ch'ora io ti chieggo. Sento nell'anima già le tue pene; coraggio e il nobile cor vincerà.

GERMONT:
Yes, cry, unfortunate lady. It is a great sacrifice that I ask. I feel your pain in my soul. Take heart, your sacrifice is noble and courageous.

VIOLETTA:
Or imponete!

VIOLETTA:
Tell me what to do!

GERMONT:
Non amarlo ditegli.

GERMONT:
Tell him that you no longer love him.

VIOLETTA::
Nol crederà.

VIOLETTA:
He won't believe it.

GERMONT:
Partite.

GERMONT:
Then just leave him.

VIOLETTA:
Seguirammi.

VIOLETTA:
He'll follow me.

GERMONT:
Allor....

GERMONT:
And so....

VIOLETTA:
Qual figlia m'abbracciate forte così sarò. Tra breve ei vi fia reso, ma afflitto oltre ogni dire. A suo conforto di colò volerete.

VIOLETTA:
I've made up my mind. Embrace me like a daughter. Soon you will have him back, but he will be so brokenhearted. You must be here to console him.

GERMONT:
Che pensate?

GERMONT:
What are you planning to do?

VIOLETTA:
Sapendol, v'opporreste al pensier mio.

VIOLETTA:
If I told you, you wouldn't agree.

GERMONT:
Generosa! E per voi che far poss'io?

GERMONT:
Noble lady. How can I repay you?

VIOLETTA:
Morrò! La mia memoria non fia ch'ei maledica, se le mie pene orribili vi sia chi almen gli dica.

VIOLETTA:
I will die! My sins cannot be erased, but let everyone know the horrible agony I have suffered.

GERMONT:
No, generosa, vivere, e lieta voi dovrete, mercè di queste lagrime dal cielo un giorno avrete.

GERMONT:
No, generous lady, you must live and enjoy life. One day Heaven will reward you for all the tears you have shed.

VIOLETTA:
Conosca il sacrifizio ch'io consumai d'amor che sarà suo fin l'ultimo sospiro del mio cor.

VIOLETTA:
One day Alfredo should know the sacrifice that I made for him, and that with my last breath, I loved only him.

GERMONT:
Premiato il sacrifizio sarà del vostro amor; d'un opra così nobile sarete fiera allor.

GERMONT:
Be proud and noble. You shall be rewarded for the supreme sacrifice of your love.

VIOLETTA:
Qui giunge alcun. Partite!

VIOLETTA:
Someone is coming. Please go!

GERMONT:
Ah, grato v'è il cor mio!

GERMONT:
I am most grateful to you!

VIOLETTA:
Non ci vedrem più forse.

VIOLETTA:
We may never see each other again.

A DUE:
Siate felice. Addio!

BOTH: *(embracing each other)*
Be happy. Farewell!

Germont exits into the garden.

VIOLETTA:
Dammi tu forza, o cielo!

VIOLETTA:
Oh God, please give me strength!

ANNINA:
Mi richiedeste?

ANNINA:
You rang for me?

Violetta sits at a writing table to respond to Flora's invitation. She rings for Annina, who looks at the address in surprise.

VIOLETTA:
Sì, reca tu stessa questo foglio. Silenzio va' all'istante.

VIOLETTA:
Yes. I want you to deliver this letter. Don't say anything! Go at once!

Ed ora si scriva a lui. Che gli dirò? Chi men darà il coraggio?

And now I must write to Alfredo. What shall I say? Who will give me the courage?

As Violetta seals the letter, Alfredo suddenly appears.

ALFREDO:
Che fai?

ALFREDO:
What are you doing?

VIOLETTA:
Nulla.

VIOLETTA: *(concealing the letter)*
Nothing.

ALFREDO:
Scrivevi?

ALFREDO:
Were you writing?

VIOLETTA:
Sì, no.

VIOLETTA: *(Violetta is disturbed)*
Yes, no.

ALFREDO:
Qual turbamento! A chi scrivevi?

ALFREDO:
You're so disturbed! To whom were you writing?

VIOLETTA:
A te.

VIOLETTA:
To you.

ALFREDO:
Dammi quel foglio!

ALFREDO:
Give me that letter!

VIOLETTA:
No, per ora.

VIOLETTA:
No, not now.

ALFREDO:
Mi perdona, son io preoccupato.

ALFREDO: *(apologetically)*
Forgive me, I'm not myself.

VIOLETTA:
Che fu?

VIOLETTA:
What is it?

ALFREDO:
Giunse mio padre.

ALFREDO:
My father is coming.

VIOLETTA:
Lo vedesti?

VIOLETTA:
Have you seen him?

ALFREDO:
Ah no: severo scritto mi lasciava però l'attendo, t'amerà in vederti.

ALFREDO:
No, but he left me a harsh note and wants to see me. He'll love you when he sees you.

VIOLETTA:
Ch'ei qui non mi sorprenda. Lascia che m'allontani tu lo calma. Ai piedi suoi mi getterò divisi ei più non ne vorrà sarem felici. Perchè tu m'ami, Alfredo, non è vero?

VIOLETTA: *(agitated)*
Oh, he must not find me here! I'll leave while you meet with him. Then I'll throw myself at his feet. Surely he wouldn't want to separate us now. We shall be happy, for you do love me Alfredo, right?

ALFREDO:
O, quanto. Perchè piangi?

ALFREDO:
Oh so very much. But why are you crying?

VIOLETTA:
Di lagrime avea d'uopo or son tranquilla. Lo vedi? Ti sorrido. Sarò là, tra quei fior presso a te sempre.

VIOLETTA:
My heart was so heavy, but I am calm now. You see? I can even smile. I shall be there, in the garden, always near you.

Amami Alfredo, quant'io t'amo. Addio.

Love me Alfredo, love me as much as I love you. Goodbye.

Violetta rushes out into the garden.

ALFREDO:
Ah, vive sol quel core all'amor mio!

ALFREDO:
Ah, that dear heart lives only for my love!

Alfredo sits down and begins reading a book.
He then rises and looks at the clock on the mantel.

È tardi: ed oggi forse più non verrà mio padre.

It's late. Maybe my father isn't coming today.

GIUSEPPE: La signora è partita l'attendeva un calesse, e sulla via già corre di Parigi. Annina pure prima di lei spariva.	**GIUSEPPE:** *(hurrying in)* The mistress has left in a carriage, en route to Paris. Annina left earlier.
ALFREDO: Il so, ti calma.	**ALFREDO:** I know all that. Be calm.
GIUSEPPE: (Che vuol dir ciò?)	**GIUSEPPE:** *(aside)* (What does all this mean?) *(Giuseppe exits)*
ALFREDO: Va forse d'ogni avere ad affrettar la perdita. Ma Annina lo impedirà.	**ALFREDO:** *(aside)* She's gone, ruining herself by rushing to sell everything, but Annina will prevent her.

Germont is seen approaching from the garden.

Qualcuno è nel giardino! Chi è là?	Someone's in the garden. Who is it?
MESSAGIERO: Il signor Germont?	**MESSENGER:** *(at the door)* Monsieur Germont?
ALFREDO: Son io.	**ALFREDO:** That's me.
MESSAGIERO: Una dama da un cocchio, per voi, di qua non lunge, mi diede questo scritto.	**MESSENGER:** A short while ago, a lady in a carriage gave me this letter to give to you.
ALFREDO: Di Violetta. Perchè son io commosso! A raggiungerla forse ella m'invita. Io tremo! Oh ciel! Coraggio!	**ALFREDO:** It's from Violetta. Why am I so unnerved? Perhaps she's asking me to join her. I'm trembling! Oh Heaven! Be strong!
"Alfredo, al giungervi di questo foglio"	"Alfredo, by the time you read this letter"

As he cries out in shock, he finds himself facing his father.
Father and son embrace.

Ah! Padre mio!	Oh! Father!

GERMONT:
Mio figlio! Oh, quanto soffri! Tergi, ah, tergi il pianto ritorna di tuo padre orgoglio e vanto.

GERMONT:
My son! What suffering! But stop crying and return to be your father's honor and pride.

Di Provenza il mar, il suol, chi dal cor ti cancello? Al natio fulgente sol, qual destino ti furò? O rammenta pur nel duol, ch'ivi gioia a te brillò; e che pace colà sol, su te splendere ancor può.

Are the land and sea of Provence erased from your memory? Wasn't its radiant sun your destiny? Oh remember that you knew happiness there. May peace again fall on all your sorrows.

Dio mi guidò! Ah! Il tuo vecchio genitor, tu non sai quanto soffrì. Te lontano, di squallor il suo tetto si coprì. Ma se alfin ti trovo ancor, se in me speme non fallì, se la voce dell'onor, in te appien non ammutì, Dio m'esaudì! Nè rispondi d'un padre all'affetto?

God led me here! Oh, how your old father has suffered since you brought shame and grief upon our home. But if I truly have found my son again, and the voice of honor is still in you, then God has granted my will! Are you unresponsive to your father's affection?

ALFREDO:
Mille serpi divoranmi il petto!
Mi lasciate!

ALFREDO:
I am being devoured by grief!
Leave me!

GERMONT:
Lasciarti?

GERMONT:
Leave you?

ALFREDO:
(Oh vendetta!)

ALFREDO:
(Oh, vengeance!)

GERMONT:
Non più indugi; partiamo t'affretta.

GERMONT:
Stop indulging yourself. Let's leave right away.

ALFREDO:
(Ah, fu Douphol!)

ALFREDO:
(Ah, it was Douphol!)

GERMONT:
M'ascolti tu?

GERMONT:
Are you listening to me?

ALFREDO:
No!.

ALFREDO:
No!

GERMONT:
Dunque invano trovato t'avrò! No, non udrai rimproveri; copriam d'oblio il passato; l'amor che m'ha guidato, sa tutto perdonar. Vieni, i tuoi cari in giubilo con me rivedi ancora: a chi penò finora tal gioia non negar. Un padre ed una suora t'affretta a consolar.

GERMONT:
Then my efforts were futile! No, I won't reproach you, but we must forget the past. The love that guided me here has taught me to forgive everything. Come, your loved ones await you joyfully. Your father and your sister will console you.

Alfredo sees Flora's invitation on the table and reads it.

ALFREDO:
Ah! Ell'è alla festa! volisi. L'offesa a vendicar.

ALFREDO:
Ah! She's left to go to Flora's party! Such an insult must be avenged.

GERMONT:
Che dici? Ah, ferma!

GERMONT:
What did you say? Stop it!

Alfredo rushes out, followed by his father.

End of Act II - Scene 1

Act II - Scene 2

The salon of Flora's Paris mansion, elegantly furnished and brilliantly illuminated. Immediately present are Flora, the Marquis, and Doctor Grenvil.

FLORA: Avrem lieta di maschere la notte: n'è duce il viscontino. Violetta ed Alfredo anco invitai.	**FLORA:** For entertainment this evening, we have masqueraders, a gift from the Viscount. Violetta and Alfredo are also invited.
MARCHESE: La novità ignorate? Violetta e Germont sono disgiunti.	**MARQUIS:** Don't you know the news? Violetta and Alfredo have separated.
DOTTORE E FLORA: Fia vero?	**DOCTOR and FLORA:** Really?
MARCHESE: Ella verrà qui col barone.	**MARQUIS:** She's coming with the Baron.
DOTTORE: Li vidi ieri ancor, parean felici.	**DOCTOR:** I just saw them yesterday, and they seemed quite happy.
FLORA: Silenzio! Udite!	**FLORA:** Hush! Listen!
TUTTI: Giungono gli amici.	**ALL:** Our friends are arriving.

Ladies dressed as Gypsies enter.

ZINGARE: Noi siamo zingarelle venute da lontano; d'ognuno sulla mano leggiamo l'avvenir. Se consultiam le stelle null'avvi a noi d'oscuro, e i casi del futuro possiamo altrui predir.	**GYPSIES:** We are gypsies who have come from afar. We read the future from your hand. When we consult the stars, all of your secrets are revealed so we can predict your future.

One gypsy examines Flora's hand.

Vediamo! Voi, signora, rivali alquante avete.	Let's see now! You, my lady, have many rivals.

Another gypsy reads the hand of the Marquis.

Voi, Marchese, voi non siete model di fedeltà.	You, Marquis, are not a model of fidelity.
FLORA: Fate il galante ancora? Ben, vò me la paghiate	**FLORA:** *(to the Marquis)* Are you still philandering? You'll pay me dearly for this!
MARCHESE: Che dianci vi pensate? L'accusa è falsità.	**MARQUIS:** *(to Flora)* You can't be serious? What she says is not true.
FLORA: La volpe lascia il pelo, non abbandona il vizio Marchese mio, giudizio o vi farò pentir.	**FLORA:** The fox may leave its hair, but never its manners. Dear Marquis, be careful or I'll make you regret it.
TUTTI: Su via, si stenda un velo cui fatti del passato; già quel ch'è stato è stato. Badate all'avvenir.	**ALL:** Away then, forget past mistakes. What is done is done. Pay attention to the future.

Flora and the Marquis shake hands. Gastone and other guests arrive, some disguised as Spanish Matadors and Picadors.

GASTONE E MATTADORI: Di Madride noi siam mattadori, siamo i prodi del circo dè tori, testè giunti a godere del chiasso che a Parigi si fa pel bue grasso; è una storia, se udire vorrete, quali amanti noi siamo saprete.	**GASTONE and MATADORS:** We're from Madrid, and are the pride of the bullring. We've come to Paris to share your enjoyment, and if you would listen, we'll tell you the story of what great lovers we are.
GLI ALTRI: Sì, sì, bravi: narrate, narrate! Con piacere l'udremo.	**ALL:** Yes, yes, brave ones, tell us! We'd love to hear it.
GASTONE E MATTADORI: Ascoltate. È Piquillo un bel gagliardo biscaglino mattador: forte il braccio, fiero il guardo, delle giostre egli è signor.	**GASTONE and MATADORS:** Listen! Our Piquillo, the handsome Matador comes from Biscay. With his strong arms and proud look, he is the hero of the bullring.

D'andalusa giovinetta follemente innamorò; ma la bella ritrosetta così al giovane parlò: cinque tori in un sol giorno vò vederti ad atterrar; e, se vinci, al tuo ritorno mano e cor ti vò donar.
Sì, gli disse, e il mattadore, alle giostre mosse il piè; cinque tori, vincitore sull'arena egli stendè.

A fair Andalusian maiden fell passionately in love with him.She told him: "I personally want to see you slay five fierce bulls within one day, and if you succeed, I will give you my heart and hand."
The Matador agreed, walked into the ring, and triumphantly slew five bulls in the arena.

GLI ALTRI:
Bravo, bravo il mattadore, ben gagliardo si mostrò se alla giovane l'amore in tal guisa egli provò.

ALL:
Bravo, bravo for the Matador. He proved that he was a valiant fighter and how much he loved the young lady.

GASTONE E MATTADORI:
Poi, tra plausi, ritornato alla bella del suo cor, colse il premio desiato tra le braccia dell'amor.

GASTONE and MATADORS:
Then, amidst the applause, he knelt before his loved one, and then took his prize in his arms.

GLI ALTRI:
Con tai prove i mattadori san le belle conquistar!

ALL:
With such trials, matadors conquer beautiful women!

GASTONE E MATTADORI:
Ma qui son più miti i cori; a noi basta folleggiar.

GASTONE and MATADORS:
But here, hearts are easier to win.
But enough, let's rejoice.

TUTTI:
Sì, sì, allegri or pria tentiamo della sorte il vario umor; la palestra dischiudiamo agli audaci giuocator.

ALL:
Yes, let's rejoice and be happy! But first let's test our luck. Let's go to the tables to try our chances.

As men begin to play at the gaming tables,
Alfredo arrives.

TUTTI:
Alfredo! Voi!

ALL:
Alfredo! You!

ALFREDO:
Sì, amici.

ALFREDO:
Yes, my friends.

FLORA: Violetta?	**FLORA:** Where is Violetta?
ALFREDO: Non ne so.	**ALFREDO:** I don't know.
TUTTI: Ben disinvolto! Bravo! Or via, giuocar si può.	**ALL:** He doesn't seem to care. Bravo! Then let's go and play.

Gastone cuts the cards. Alfredo joins the game.
Violetta enters, escorted by Baron Douphol.

FLORA: Qui desiata giungi.	**FLORA:** *(to Violetta)* We've been anxiously waiting for you.
VIOLETTA: Cessi al cortese invito.	**VIOLETTA:** I couldn't' resist your charming invitation.
FLORA: Grata vi son, barone, d'averlo pur gradito.	**FLORA:** I'm grateful that you and the Baron accepted.
BARONE: (Germont è qui! Il vedete!)	**BARON:** *(whispering to Violetta)* (Germont is here! Do you see him?)
VIOLETTA: (Ciel! gli è vero). Il vedo.	**VIOLETTA:** *(aside)* (Heaven! It's true.) I see him.
BARONE: Da voi non un sol detto si volga a questo Alfredo.	**BARON:** You're not to say a word to this Alfredo.
VIOLETTA: (Ah, perchè venni, incauta! Pietà di me, gran Dio!)	**VIOLETTA:** *(aside)* (Ah, why did I come. So stupid of me! Dear God, have mercy on me!)
FLORA: Meco t'assidi: narrami quai novità vegg'io?	**FLORA:** *(to Violetta)* Sit here beside me. Tell me about this news I'm hearing?

While Flora and Violetta converse quietly, Alfredo plays in the card game.

ALFREDO:
Un quattro!

ALFREDO:
A four!

GASTONE:
Ancora hai vinto!

GASTONE:
You win again!

ALFREDO:
Sfortuna nell'amore Vale fortuna al giuoco!

ALFREDO:
Unlucky in love, lucky in the game!

TUTTI:
È sempre vincitore!

ALL:
He always wins!

ALFREDO:
Oh, vincerò stasera; e l'oro guadagnato poscia a goder tra campi ritornerò beato.

ALFREDO:
Oh, I'll win tonight, and as before, I'll spend my winnings on country pleasures.

FLORA:
Solo?

FLORA:
Alone?

ALFREDO:
No, no, con tale che vi fu meco ancor, poi mi sfuggia.

ALFREDO:
No, no, but with the person who had earlier left me.

VIOLETTA:
(Mio Dio!)

VIOLETTA:
(Dear God!)

GASTONE:
Pietà di lei!

GASTONE: *(to Alfredo, indicating Violetta)* Have mercy on her!

BARONE:
Signor!

BARON: *(to Alfredo wrathfully)*
Sir!

VIOLETTA::
Frenatevi, o vi lascio.

VIOLETTA: *(whispering to the Baron)*
Behave yourself or I'll leave you!

ALFREDO:
Barone, m'appellaste?

ALFREDO. *(sarcastically)*
Baron, were you talking to me?

BARONE:
Siete in sì gran fortuna, che al giuoco mi tentaste.

BARON: *(with irony)*
You're having such extraordinary luck that I'm tempted to challenge you.

ALFREDO: Sì? La disfida accetto.	**ALFREDO:** Really? I accept the challenge.
VIOLETTA: (Che fia? morir mi sento.)	**VIOLETTA:** *(aside)* (What will happen? I feel like dying.)
BARONE: Cento luigi a destra.	**BARON:** *(at the gaming tables)* A hundred louis to the right.
ALFREDO: Ed alla manca cento.	**ALFREDO:** And a hundred to the left.
GASTONE: Un asse un fante hai vinto!	**GASTONE:** *(dealing)* An ace, a jack *(to Alfredo)* You've won!
BARONE: Il doppio?	**BARON:** Do you want to double it?
ALFREDO: Il doppio sia.	**ALFREDO:** I'll double it.
GASTONE: Un quattro, un sette.	**GASTONE:** *(dealing)* A four, a seven.
TUTTI: Ancora!	**ALL:** Again!
ALFREDO: Pur la vittoria è mia!	**ALFREDO:** I've won again!
CORO: Bravo davver! La sorte è tutta per Alfredo!	**CHORUS:** Bravo, really! Alfredo has all the luck!
FLORA: Del villeggiar la spesa farà il baron, già il vedo.	**FLORA:** I see now that it's the Baron who'll be paying for Alfredo's country expenses.
ALFREDO: Seguite pur.	**ALFREDO:** *(to the Baron)* Go on.
SERVO: La cena è pronta.	**SERVANT:** Dinner is served.

FLORA:
Andiamo.

FLORA:
Let's go.

ALFREDO:
Se continuar v'aggrada.

ALFREDO: *(aside to the Baron)*
If you'd like to continue.

BARONE:
Per ora nol possiamo: più tardi la rivincita.

BARON:
Not right now, but later we'll have the final rematch.

ALFREDO:
Al gioco che vorrete.

ALFREDO:
At whatever game you choose.

BARONE:
Seguiam gli amici; poscia.

BARON:
Later, but now let's follow our friends.

ALFREDO:
Sarò qual bramerete.

ALFREDO:
Whatever you wish.

The guests enter the dining room. Violetta, much agitated, returns to the salon, and is soon followed by Alfredo.

VIOLETTA:
Invitato a qui seguirmi. Verrà desso? vorra udirmi? Ei verrà, che l'odio atroce puote in lui più di mia voce.

VIOLETTA:
I sent for him. Will he meet me? Will he listen to me? He will come because his hatred for me is stronger than my love for him.

ALFREDO:
Mi chiamaste? che bramate?

ALFREDO:
Did you send for me? What do you want?

VIOLETTA:
Questi luoghi abbandonate. Un periglio vi sovrasta.

VIOLETTA:
I beg you to leave this place. You're in great danger.

ALFREDO:
Ah, comprendo! Basta, basta e sì vile mi credete?

ALFREDO:
Oh, now I understand! It is enough. Do you think I am a coward?

VIOLETTA:
Ah no, mai!

VIOLETTA:
Oh, no, of course not!

ALFREDO:
Ma che temete?

ALFREDO:
Then why are you so afraid?

VIOLETTA:
Temo sempre del Barone.

VIOLETTA:
It's the Baron I'm afraid of.

ALFREDO:
È tra noi mortal quistione s'ei cadrà per mano mia un sol colpo vi torrì a coll'amante il protettore. V'atterrisce tal sciagura?

ALFREDO:
It's true we have a deadly feud. If I would kill him you would lose both lover and protector in one blow. Is that what you're so afraid of?

VIOLETTA:
Ma s'ei fosse l'uccisore? Ecco l'unica sventura ch'io pavento a me fatale!

VIOLETTA:
Oh, but what if he kills you? That would by a most fatal misfortune for me!

ALFREDO:
La mia morte! Che ven cale?

ALFREDO:
My death! What does that mean to you?

VIOLETTA:
Deh, partite, e sull'istante!

VIOLETTA:
Go, I beg you! Leave right now!

ALFREDO:
Partirò, ma giura innante che dovunque seguirai i miei passi.

ALFREDO:
I'll leave, but only if you swear to come with me.

VIOLETTA:
Ah, no, giammai!

VIOLETTA:
Oh no, never!

ALFREDO:
No! Giammai?

ALFREDO:
No! Never?

VIOLETTA::
Và, sciagurato. Scorda un nome ch'è infamato. Va mi lascia sul momento di fuggirti un giuramento sacro io feci.

VIOLETTA:
Go, unfortunate one. Forget my disgraced name and leave me immediately. I have sworn a sacred oath to give you up.

ALFREDO:
E chi potea?

ALFREDO:
And who wanted that?

VIOLETTA:
Chi diritto pien ne avea.

VIOLETTA:
One whose honor was beyond question.

ALFREDO:
Fu Douphol?

ALFREDO:
Was it Douphol?

VIOLETTA::
Sì!

VIOLETTA: *(with supreme effort)*
Yes!

ALFREDO:
Dunque l'ami?

ALFREDO:
Then you love him?

VIOLETTA:
Ebben l'amo!

VIOLETTA:
Yes, I love him!

ALFREDO:
Or tutti a me.

ALFREDO: *(impetuously to the guests)*
Everybody come here!

TUTTI:
Ne appellaste? Che volete?

ALL:
Did you call us? What do you want?

ALFREDO:
Questa donna conoscete?

ALFREDO: *(pointing to Violetta)*
Do you all know this woman?

TUTTI:
Chi? Violetta?

ALL:
Who? Violetta?

ALFREDO:
Che facesse non sapete?

ALFREDO:
Do you know what she has done?

VIOLETTA:
Ah, taci.

VIOLETTA:
Oh, spare me.

TUTTI:
No.

ALL:
No.

ALFREDO:
Ogni suo aver tal femmina per amor
mio sperdea. Io cieco, vile, misero,
tutto accettar potea.
Ma è tempo ancora! tergermi da tanta
macchia bramo.
Qui testimoni vi chiamo che qui pagata io l'ho.

ALFREDO:
This woman spent all that she owned
on her lover. I was blind, vile, foolish,
and accepted it all.
But there's still time to clear myself
from this shame and dishonor.
Witness as I pay my debts to her.

Alfredo violently flings his winnings at Violetta. She faints in Flora's arms. Suddenly, Germont appears. He has heard Alfredo curse Violetta.

TUTTI:
Oh, infamia orribile tu commettesti! Un cor sensibile così uccidesti! Di donne ignobile insultator, di qui allontanati, ne desti orror.

ALL:
You have committed a dreadful injustice! With your wretched insult you have broken a tender heart! Leave! Your behavior horrifies us.

GERMONT:
Di sprezzo degno se stesso rende chi pur nell'ira la donna offende.
Dove'è mio figlio? Più non lo vedo: in te più Alfredo trovar non so.
(Io sol fra tanti so qual virtude di quella misera il sen racchiude io so che l'ama, che gli è fedele, eppur, crudele, tacer dovrò!)

GERMONT: *(reproachfully)*
For any man who offends a woman like that, there is insufficient disdain.
Where is my son? I no longer see him.
You, Alfredo, are not my son.
(Aside) (I alone know what a virtuous heart beats in that woman's unhappy soul, and how loving and true she is. It is cruel that I cannot reveal the truth!)

ALFREDO:
Ah sì che feci! Ne sento orrore. Gelosa smania, deluso amore mi strazia l'alma più non ragiono.
Da lei perdono, più non avrò. Volea fuggirla non ho potuto! Dall'ira spinto son qui venuto! Or che lo sdegno ho disfogato, me sciagurato! Rimorso n'ho.

ALFREDO: *(Aside.)*
What have I done? I am horrified! My action appalls me! The raging jealousy in my soul is what destroyed my reason.
She won't forgive me. I wanted to flee from her, but I could not. My rage led me to come here; a disdain that turned to madness. I am so ashamed, and I feel such remorse.

VIOLETTA:
Alfredo, Alfredo, di questo core non puoi comprendere tutto l'amore; tu non conosci che fino a prezzo del tuo disprezzo, provato io l'ho!
Ma verrò giorno in che il saprai com'io t'amassi confesserai Dio dai rimorsi ti salvi allora; io spenta ancora pur t'amerò.

VIOLETTA:
Alfredo, Alfredo, you don't know how much I love you! You'll never know that I created your contempt in order to prove my love for you.
But some day you'll know how much I loved you, and then you will confess your remorse to God, who will redeem you. But even in death, I will always love you.

BARONE:
A questa donna l'atroce insulto qui tutti offese, ma non inulto fia tanto oltraggio, provar vi voglio che tanto orgoglio fiaccar saprò.

BARON: *(aside to Alfredo)*
We've all heard how outrageously you have insulted this lady, and we're all deeply offended. I want to redeem her pride, and I know how to do it.

TUTTI:
Ah, quanto peni! Ma pur fa core qui soffre ognuno del tuo dolore; fra cari amici qui sei soltanto; rasciuga il pianto che t'inondò.

ALL: *(to Violetta)*
Oh, such sorrow! But be comforted that we have compassion for your anguish. Dry your tears Violetta, for you are not alone, but among loving friends.

Germont leads Alfredo out, but not before the Baron challenges Alfredo to a duel.

End of Act II - Scene 2

Act III

One month later. Violetta's bedroom. Violetta is sleeping; Annina dozes in a chair.

VIOLETTA: Annina?	**VIOLETTA:** *(awaking)* Annina?
ANNINA: Comandate?	**ANNINA:** You called me?
VIOLETTA: Dormivi, poveretta?	**VIOLETTA:** Were you asleep, poor girl?
ANNINA: Sì, perdonate.	**ANNINA:** Yes. Forgive me.
VIOLETTA: Dammi d'acqua un sorso. Osserva, è pieno il giorno?	**VIOLETTA:** Please give me a drink of water. Look, is it morning already?
ANNINA: Son sett'ore.	**ANNINA:** It is seven o'clock.
VIOLETTA: Dà accesso a un po' di luce.	**VIOLETTA:** Let a little light in.
ANNINA: Il signor di Grenvil!	**ANNINA:** *(opens the shutters)* Oh, there's Mr. Grenvil!
VIOLETTA: Oh, il vero amico! Alzar mi vo' m'aita.	**VIOLETTA:** Oh, he's such a true friend! Help me. I want to get up.

She rises from the bed with difficulty, and then walks unsteadily toward a chair. Doctor Grenvil arrives.

VIOLETTA: Quanta bontà pensaste a me per tempo!	**VIOLETTA:** How good of you to think of me so often!

DOTTORE:
Or, come vi sentite?

DOCTOR: *(feels her pulse)*
How are you feeling now?

VIOLETTA:
Soffre il mio corpo, ma tranquilla ho l'alma. Mi confortò iersera un pio ministro. Religione è sollievo a sofferenti.

VIOLETTA:
My body suffers, but my soul is at peace. Last night a priest comforted me greatly. Religion brings relief to the suffering.

DOTTORE:
E questa notte?

DOCTOR:
And how did you sleep?

VIOLETTA:
Ebbi tranquillo il sonno.

VIOLETTA:
I slept quite peacefully.

DOTTORE:
Coraggio adunque la convalescenza non è lontana.

DOCTOR:
Have courage then. You'll soon be well again.

VIOLETTA:
Oh, la bugia pietosa a medici è concessa!

VIOLETTA:
Oh, a pious lie is a doctor's prerogative!

DOTTORE:
Addio a più tardi.

DOCTOR: *(clasps her hand)*
Goodbye. I will see you later.

VIOLETTA:
Non mi scordate.

VIOLETTA:
Don't forget me.

ANNINA:
Come va, signore?

ANNINA: *(whispering to the Doctor)* How is she, Doctor?

DOTTORE:
La tisi non le accorda che poche ore.

DOCTOR:
She has only a few hours to live.

The Doctor leaves.

ANNINA:
Or fate cor!

ANNINA:
Cheer up!

VIOLETTA:
Giorno di festa è questo?

VIOLETTA:
Is today a holiday?

ANNINA:
Tutta Parigi impazza è carnevale.

ANNINA:
All Paris is going mad because of carnival.

VIOLETTA:
Ah, nel comun tripudio, sallo il cielo quanti infelici soffron!
Quale somma v'ha in quello stipo?

VIOLETTA:
In all this gaiety, Heaven only knows how many poor creatures are suffering! How much money do we have in that cupboard?

ANNINA:
Venti luigi.

ANNINA:
Twenty louis.

VIOLETTA:
Dieci ne reca ai poveri tu stessa.

VIOLETTA:
Go out and distribute ten among the poor.

ANNINA:
Poco rimanevi allora.

ANNINA:
Then you'll have very little left.

VIOLETTA:
Oh, mi sarà bastante;
cerca poscia mie lettere.

VIOLETTA:
Oh, it will be enough for me!
Please bring me my mail.

ANNINA:
Ma voi?

ANNINA:
But you?

VIOLETTA:
Nulla occorrà sollecita, se puoi.

VIOLETTA:
I don't need anything, only don't be long.
(Annina exits)

Violetta reads the letter that she received from Giorgio Germont.

"Teneste la promessa la disfida ebbe luogo! il barone fu ferito, però migliora Alfredo è in stranio suolo; il vostro sacrifizio io stesso gli ho svelato; egli a voi tornerà pel suo perdono; io pur verrò curatevi meritate un avvenir migliore — Giorgio Germont."

"You kept your promise. The duel took place. The Baron was wounded, but he is now recovering. Alfredo is out of the country. I myself told him about your sacrifice. He will be coming to you to ask your forgiveness. I too will come to see you. Get well. You deserve a better future. Giorgio Germont."

È tardi! Attendo, attendo nè a me giungon mai!

How late it is! I wait and wait but they never come!

Violetta gazes at herself in the mirror.

Oh, come son mutata! Ma il dottore a sperar pure m'esorta! Ah, con tal morbo ogni speranza è morta.

Oh, how I've changed! And yet the Doctor told me that there is hope! Oh, with such an illness, the only hope is death.

Addio, del passato bei sogni ridenti.
Le rose del volto già son pallenti;
l'amore d'Alfredo pur esso mi manca,
conforto, sostegno dell'anima stanca.

Farewell, bright memories of the past.
My rosy cheeks are pale. I miss
Alfredo's love, whose comfort
sustained my weary soul.

Ah, della traviata sorridi al desio; a lei, deh, perdona; tu accoglila, o Dio, or tutto finì. Le gioie, i dolori tra poco avran fine, la tomba ai mortali di tutto è confine! Non lagrima o fiore avrà la mia fossa, non croce col nome che copra quest'ossa! Ah, della traviata sorridi al desio; a lei, deh, perdona; tu accoglila, o Dio. Or tutto finì!

Oh God, grant pardon to this fallen woman for whom life is ending. The joys and pains will soon be over, and the tomb of this mortal will be covered.
There will be no tears or flowers, and no name on the cross that covers these remains! Oh God, grant pardon to this fallen woman. All is over!

CORO DI MASCHERE:
Largo al quadrupede sir della festa, di fiori e pampini cinto la testa. Largo al più docile d'ogni cornuto, di corni e pifferi abbia il saluto.

CHORUS: *(offstage)*
Make way for the lord of the festivities, the most docile of horned beasts. He is adorned with flowers and vine-leaves on his head. We salute him with pipe and horn.

Parigini, date passo al trionfo del bue grasso. L'Asia, nè l'Africa vide il più bello, vanto ed orgoglio d'ogni macello allegre maschere, pazzi garzoni, tutti plauditelo con canti e suoni!
Parigini, date passo al trionfo del Bue grasso.

Come Parisians, make way for the celebration of the fat bull. Asia or Africa have no equal. Happy masquer-aders and wild children, boasting with pride, greet and cheer him with song and applause!
Come Parisians, make way for the celebration of the fat bull.

ANNINA: Signora!	**ANNINA:** *(returning excitedly)* Madam!
VIOLETTA: Che t'accade?	**VIOLETTA:** What is it?
ANNINA: Quest'oggi, è vero? Vi sentite meglio?	**ANNINA:** Are you really feeling better today?
VIOLETTA: Sì, perchè?	**VIOLETTA:** Yes, but why do you ask?
ANNINA: D'esser calma promettete?	**ANNINA:** Do you promise not to get excited?
VIOLETTA: Sì, che vuoi dirmi?	**VIOLETTA:** Yes, what do you want to tell me?
ANNINA: Prevenir vi volli una gioia improvvisa.	**ANNINA:** I want to prepare you for a joyous surprise.
VIOLETTA: Una gioia! dicesti?	**VIOLETTA:** Did you say a joyous surprise?
ANNINA: Sì, o signora.	**ANNINA:** Yes, Madam.
VIOLETTA: Alfredo! Ah, tu il vedesti? Ei vien! L'affretta!	**VIOLETTA:** It's Alfredo! You've seen him? He's coming! Hurry!

Annina gestures, and then opens the door.

VIOLETTA: Alfredo!	**VIOLETTA:** *(runs to the door)* Alfredo!

Violetta and Alfredo fall into each other's arms.

Amato Alfredo!	My beloved Alfredo!
ALFREDO: Mia Violetta! Colpevol sono so tutto, o cara.	**ALFREDO:** My Violetta! It's all my fault, my love. I know everything now.

VIOLETTA:
Io so che alfine reso mi sei!

VIOLETTA:
I only know that you've come back to me.

ALFREDO:
Da questo palpito s'io t'ami impara, senza te esistere più non potrei.

ALFREDO:
My heartbeats reveal all my devotion. It is only with you that life is worth living.

VIOLETTA:
Ah, s'anco in vita m'hai ritrovata, credi che uccidere non può il dolor.

VIOLETTA:
One does not die from sorrow. Look at me, I'm rejuvenated.

ALFREDO:
Scorda l'affanno, donna adorata, a me perdona e al genitor.

ALFREDO:
My love, forget your sorrow, and forgive me and my father.

VIOLETTA:
Ch'io ti perdoni? La rea son io: ma solo amore tal mi rendè.

VIOLETTA:
Forgive you, Alfredo? If my love for you can be blamed, then it was my fault.

A DUE:
Null'uomo o demone, angelo mio, mai più staccarti potrà da me.
Parigi, o cara/o noi lasceremo, la vita uniti trascorreremo: se' corsi affanni compenso avrai, la mia/tua salute rifiorirà. Sospiro e luce tu mi sarai, tutto il futuro ne arriderà.

BOTH:
My angel, neither man nor demon will ever tear us away from each other.
We'll leave Paris, my love, and our life together will change. Sorrow will be replaced by happiness. My/your health will improve and you will light up my life. Our future together will be full of happiness.

VIOLETTA:
Ah, non più, a un tempio Alfredo, andiamo, del tuo ritorno grazie rendiamo.

VIOLETTA:
Oh, no more! Alfredo, let's go to church to offer our thanks for your return.

Violetta has a sudden spasm.

ALFREDO:
Tu impallidisci!

ALFREDO:
You've turned pale!

VIOLETTA:
È nulla, sai! Gioia improvvisa non entra mai senza turbarlo in mesto core.

VIOLETTA:
It's nothing, really. Sudden happiness can always affect a sad heart.

Violetta sinks down into a chair.

ALFREDO: Gran Dio! Violetta!	**ALFREDO:** Oh God! Violetta!
VIOLETTA: È il mio malore fu debolezza! ora son forte. Vedi! Sorrido.	**VIOLETTA:** It's my illness. I felt myself growing faint. Now I'm stronger. See, I'm smiling.
ALFREDO: (Ahi, cruda sorte!)	**ALFREDO:** *(aside)* (Oh, cruel fate!)
VIOLETTA: Fu nulla. Annina, dammi a vestire.	**VIOLETTA:** It was nothing. Annina, give me something to wear.
ALFREDO: Adesso? Attendi!	**ALFREDO:** Right now? Wait awhile!

Violetta tries to dress, but becomes faint.

VIOLETTA: No voglio uscire.	**VIOLETTA:** No. I want to go out.

She throws the dress aside, and falls back into the chair.

Gran Dio! Non posso!	Oh God, I can't!
ALFREDO: (Cielo! che vedo! Va pel dottor.	**ALFREDO:** *(to Annina)* Heavens! What's happened? Get the doctor right away.
VIOLETTA: Digli che Alfredo è ritornato all'amor mio.Digli che vivere ancor vogl'io.	**VIOLETTA:** *(to Annina)* Tell him that Alfredo has returned to me. Tell him that I desperately want to live. *(Annina exits)*
Ma se tornando non m'hai salvato, a niuno in terra salvarmi è dato.	But if by coming back you have not saved me, then nothing can save me.
Gran Dio! Morir sì giovane, io che penato ho tanto! Morir sì presso a tergere il mio sì lungo pianto!	Oh God! For me to die so young, and to have suffered so much! To die when there is hope of a happier tomorrow!

Ah, dunque fu delirio la cruda mia speranza; invano di costanza armato avrò il mio cor! Alfredo! Oh! Il crudo termine serbato al nostro amor!	Therefore my fierce hope was just an illusion, a futile strengthening of my heart. Oh Alfredo, this is a cruel ending to our love!
ALFREDO: Oh mio sospiro, oh palpito, diletto del cor mio! Le mie colle tue lagrime confondere degg'io ma più che mai, deh, credilo, m'è d'uopo di costanza, Ah! Tutto alla speranza non chiudere il tuo cor.	**ALFREDO:** Oh my loved one, the ecstasy and delight of my heart! My soul shares your tears. More than ever, we must be faithful to each other, and never give up hope in our hearts.

Germont and the Doctor arrive.

GERMONT: Ah, Violetta!	**GERMONT:** Ah, Violetta!
VIOLETTA: Voi, Signor!	**VIOLETTA:** You, sir!
ALFREDO: Mio padre!	**ALFREDO:** Father!
VIOLETTA: Non mi scordaste?	**VIOLETTA:** You didn't forget me?
GERMONT: La promessa adempio a stringervi qual figlia vengo al seno, o generosa.	**GERMONT:** Generous woman, I'm fulfilling my promise to embrace you as my own child.
VIOLETTA: Ahimè, tardi giungeste! Pure, grata ven sono. Grenvil, vedete? Tra le braccia io spiro di quanti ho cari al mondo.	**VIOLETTA:** Alas! You've come too late! But still, I am grateful. *(embraces him)* Do you see, Grenvil, I'll be dying in the arms of those I hold dearest in the world.
GERMONT: Che mai dite? (Oh cielo è ver!)	**GERMONT:** *(aside)* What are you saying? (Too late, alas!)
ALFREDO: La vedi, padre mio?	**ALFREDO:** You see her, Father?

GERMONT:
Di più non lacerarmi troppo rimorso l'alma mi divora quasi fulmin m'atterra ogni suo detto oh, malcauto vegliardo! Ah, tutto il mal ch'io feci ora sol vedo!

GERMONT:
Don't torment me further! The remorse in my soul devours me. Her every word shatters me. I was a fool and only now do I see the extent of my mistakes!

Violetta opens a drawer and takes out a locket.

VIOLETTA:
Più a me t'appressa ascolta, amato Alfredo!

VIOLETTA:
Come close and listen to me, beloved Alfredo!

Prendi: quest'è l'immagine de' miei passati giorni; a rammentar ti torni colei che sì t'amò. Se una pudica vergine degli anni suoi nel fiore a te donasse il core sposa ti sia lo vò.
Le porgi questa effigie: dille che dono ell'è di chi nel ciel tra gli angeli prega per lei, per te.

Take this portrait of me from the past, as a remembrance of how much I loved you. If some day a virtuous young woman offers her heart to you, I want you to marry her.
Give her this portrait and tell her it is a gift from someone among the angels in Heaven, who prays for both of you.

ALFREDO:
No, non morrai, non dirmelo dei viver, amor mio a strazio sì terribile qui non mi trasse Iddio sì presto, ah no, dividerti morte non può da me. Ah, vivi, o un solo feretro m'accoglierà con te.

ALFREDO:
No, don't die. Don't tell me that! You shall live for me, my dear, and not die! Don't doom me to such cruel misery! Live, or I will join you in death.

GERMONT:
Cara, sublime vittima d'un disperato amore. Perdonami lo strazio recato al tuo bel core.

GERMONT:
Dear one, sublime victim of despairing love, forgive me for the anguish I caused you.

GERMONT, DOTTORE E ANNINA:
Finché avrà il ciglio lacrime io piangerò per te vola a beati spiriti; Iddio ti chiama a sè.

GERMONT, DOCTOR and ANNINA:
I will cry and mourn forever, because you left us for the blessed spirits. God calls you to Him.

VIOLETTA:
È strano!

VIOLETTA:
How strange I feel!

Violetta rises, her strength seemingly renewed.

TUTTI:
Che?

ALL:
What is happening?

VIOLETTA:
Cessarono gli spasmi del dolore. In me rinasce m'agita insolito vigore! Ah! io ritorno a vivere.
Oh gioia!

VIOLETTA:
The spasms from the pain have ceased. I feel reborn with an unusual resurgence of strength! Oh! I will live. Oh what joy!

(Violetta falls back)

TUTTI:
O cielo! Muor!

ALL:
Oh Heavens, she is dying!

ALFREDO:
Violetta!

ALFREDO:
Violetta!

ANNINA E GERMONT:
Oh Dio, soccorrasi!

ALL:
Oh God, save her!

DOTTORE:
È spenta!

DOCTOR: *(after feeling her pulse)*
She's dead!

TUTTI:
Oh mio dolor!

ALL:
Oh what unbearable grief!

FINE

END of OPERA

Discography

1928 Capsir (Violetta); Cecil (Alfredo); Galeffi (Germont);
La Scala Chorus and Orchestra;
Molajoli (Conductor)

1930 Rosza (Violetta); Ziliani (Alfredo); Borgonovo (Germont);
La Scala Chorus and Orchestra;
Sabajno (Conductor)

1946 Albanese (Violetta); Peerce (Alfredo); Merrill (Germont)
NBC Symphony Orchestra and Chorus;
Toscanini (Conductor)

1946 Guerrini (Violetta); Infantino (Alfredo); Silveri (Germont);
Rome Opera Chorus and Orchestra;
Bellezza (Conductor)

1952 Noli (Violetta); Campora (Alfredo); Tagliabue (Germont);
Rome Opera Chorus and Orchestra;
Berrettoni (Conductor);

1952 Schimenti (Violetta); Pola (Alfredo); Monachesi (Germont);
Rome Opera Chorus and Orchestra;
Ricci (Conductor)

1953 Callas (Violetta); Albanese (Alfredo); Savarese (Germont);
Turin Radio Chorus and Orchestra;
Santini (Conductor);

1954 Tebaldi (Violetta); Poggi (Alfredo); Protti (Germont);
Santa Cecilia Academy Chorus and Orchestra;
Molinari-Pradelli (Conductor)

1954 (Russian) Shumskaya (Violetta); Kozlovsky (Alfredo);
Lisitsian (Germont);
Bolshoi Theatre Chorus and Orchestra;
Orlov (Conductor)

1955 (Live performance) Callas (Violetta); di Stefano (Alfredo);
Bastianini (Germont);
La Scala Chorus and Orchestra;
Giulini (Conductor)

1955 Callas (Violetta); di Stefano (Alfredo); Bastianini (Germont);
La Scala Chorus and Orchestra;
Giulini (Conductor)

1956 Carteri (Violetta); Valletti (Alfredo); Warren (Germont);
Rome Opera Chorus and Orchestra;
Monteux (Conductor)

1956 Stella (Violetta); di Stefano (Alfredo); Gobbi (Germont);
La Scala Chorus and Orchestra;
Serafin (Conductor)

1958 Callas (Violetta); Kraus (Alfredo); Sereni (Germont);
San Carlos Opera Chorus and Orchestra;
Ghione (Conductor)

1959 De Los Angeles (Violetta); del Monte (Alfredo); Sereni (Germont);
Rome Opera Chorus and Orchestra;
Serafin (Conductor)

1960 Zeani (Violetta); Savio (Alfredo); Gorin (Germont);
Hamburg State Opera Chorus and Orchestra;
Annovazzi (Conductor)

1960 Moffo (Violetta); Tucker (Alfredo); Merrill (Germont);
Rome Opera Chorus and Orchestra;
Previtali (Conductor

1962 Scotto (Violetta); Raimondi (Alfredo); Bastianini (Germont);
La Scala Chorus and Orchestra;
Votto (Conductor)

1962 Sutherland (Violetta); Bergonzi (Alfredo); Merrill (Germont);
Florence Festival Chorus and Orchestra;
Pritchard (Conductor)

1963 (Hungarian) Déery (Violetta); Ilosfalvy (Alfredo); Palócz (Germont);
Budapest State Opera Chorus and Orchestra;
Gardelli (Conductor)

1967 Caballé (Violetta); Bergonzi (Alfredo); Milnes (Germont);
RCA Italiana Chorus and Orchestra;
Prêtre (Conductor)

1968 (Romanian) Zeani (Violetta); Buzea (Alfredo); Herlea (Germont);
Bucharest Opera Chorus and Orchestra;
Bobescu (Conductor)

1968 Lorengar (Violetta); Aragall (Alfredo); Fischer-Dieskau (Germont);
German Opera Chorus and Orchestra;
Maazel (Conductor)

1971 Sills (Violetta); Gedda (Alfredo); Panerai (Germont);
Alldis Choir, Royal Philharmonic Orchestra;
Ceccato (Conductor)

1973 Freni (Violetta); Bonisolli (Alfredo); Bruscantini (Germont);
Berlin State Opera Chorus and Orchestra;
Gardelli (Conductor)

1977 Cortrubas (Violetta); Domingo (Alfredo); Milnes (Germont);
Bavarian State Opera Chorus and Orchestra;
Carlos Kleiber (Conductor)

1979 Sutherland (Violetta); Pavarotti (Alfredo); Manuguerra (Germont);
London Opera Chorus, National Philharmonic Orchestra;
Bonynge (Conductor)

1980 Masterson (Violetta); Brecknock (Alfredo); du Plessis (Germont);
English National Opera Chorus and Orchestra;
Mackerras (Conductor)

1980 Scotto (Violetta); Kraus (Alfredo); Bruson (Germont);
Ambrosian Opera Chorus, Philharmonic Orchestra;
Muti (Conductor)

1981 Stratas (Violetta); Domingo (Alfredo); MacNeil (Germont);
Metropolitan Opera Chorus and Orchestra;
Levine (Conductor)

1989 Aliberti (Violetta); Dvorsky (Alfredo); Bruson (Germont); Fukiwara Opera Chorus, Tokyo Philharmonic Orchestra; Paternostro (Conductor)

1990 Fabbricini (Violetta); Alagna (Alfredo); Coni (Germont); Teatro alla Scala Orchestra and Chorus; Muti (Conductor)

1991 Studer (Violetta); Pavarotti (Alfredo); Pons (Germont); Metropolitan Opera Orchestra and Chorus; Levine (Conductor)

1992 Gruberova (Violetta); Shicoff (Alfredo); Zancanaro (Germont); La Fenice Orchestra and Chorus; Rizzi (Conductor)

1994 Gheorghiu (Violetta); Lopardo (Alfredo); Nucci (Germont); Royal Opera Orchestra and Chorus; Solti (Conductor)

2000 Gvazava (Violetta); Cura (Alfredo); Panerai (Germont); RAI Orchestra and Chorus; Mehta (Conductor)

2003 Delunsch (Violetta); Polenzani (Alfredo); Lucic (Germont) Orchestra and Chorus of Paris; Sado (Conductor)

Videography

SONY VHS

Fabbricini (Violetta); Alagna (Alfredo); Coni (Germont);
La Scala Chorus and Orchestra;
Muti (Conductor);
Cavani (Director and Video Director)

DECCA VHS/DVD

Gheorghiu (Violetta); Lopardo (Alfredo); Nucci (Germont);
Royal Opera House Chorus and Orchestra;
Solti (Conductor)
Eyre (Director)
Burton and Maniura (Video Directors)

PICKWICK VHS/ARTHAUS MUSIK DVD

McLaughlin (Violetta); MacNeil (Alfredo); Ellis (Germont);
Glyndebourne Choir, London Philharmonic Orchestra;
Haitink (Conductor);
Hall (Director and Video Director)

TELDEC/WANER DVD

Gruberova (Violetta); Shicoff (Alfredo); Zancanaro (Germont);
La Fenice Chorus and Orchestra;
Rizzi (Conductor);
Pizzi (Director);
Bailey (Video Director)

VAI VHS/DVD

Sills (Violetta); Price (Alfredo); Fredericks (Germont);
Wolf Trap Choir, Filene Center Orchestra;
Rudel (Conductor);
Capobianco (Director);
Browning (Video Director)

UNIVERSAL DVD

Stratas (Violetta); Domingo (Alfredo); Macneil (Germont)
Metropolitan Opera Orchestra and Chorus;
Levine (Conductor)
A Franco Zefferelli film

Dictionary of Opera and Musical Terms

Accelerando - Play the music faster, but gradually.

Adagio - At a slow or gliding tempo, not as slow as largo, but not as fast as andante.

Agitato - Restless or agitated.

Allegro - At a brisk or lively tempo, faster than andante but not as fast as presto.

Andante - A moderately slow, easy-going tempo.

Appoggiatura - An extra or embellishing note preceding a main melodic note. Usually written as a note of smaller size, it shares the time value of the main note.

Arabesque - Flourishes or fancy patterns usually applying to vocal virtuosity.

Aria - A solo song usually structured in a formal pattern. Arias generally convey reflective and introspective thoughts rather than descriptive action.

Arietta - A shortened form of aria.

Arioso - A musical passage or composition having a mixture of free recitative and metrical song.

Arpeggio - Producing the tones of a chord in succession rather than simultaneously.

Atonal - Music that is not anchored in traditional musical tonality; it does not use the diatonic scale and has no keynote or tonal center.

Ballad opera - Eighteenth-century English opera consisting of spoken dialogue and music derived from popular ballad and folksong sources. The most famous is *The Beggar's Opera,* which is a satire of the Italian opera seria.

Bar - A vertical line across the stave that divides the music into measures.

Baritone - A male singing voice ranging between bass and tenor.

Baroque - A style of artistic expression prevalent in the 17th century that is marked by the use of complex forms, bold ornamentation, and florid decoration. The Baroque period extends from approximately 1600 to 1750 and includes the works of the original creators of modern opera, the Camerata, as well as the later works by Bach and Handel.

Bass - The lowest male voice, usually divided into categories such as:

> **Basso buffo** - A bass voice that specializes in comic roles: Dr. Bartolo in Rossini's *The Barber of Seville.*
>
> **Basso cantante** - A bass voice that demonstrates melodic singing quality: King Philip in Verdi's *Don Carlos.*
>
> **Basso profundo** - the deepest, most profound, or most dramatic of bass voices: Sarastro in Mozart's *The Magic Flute.*

Bel canto - Literally, "beautiful singing." It originated in Italian opera of the 17th and 18th centuries and stressed beautiful tones produced with ease, clarity, purity, and evenness, together with an agile vocal technique and virtuosity. Bel canto flourished in the first half of the 19th century in the works of Rossini, Bellini, and Donizetti.

Cabaletta - A lively, concluding portion of an aria or duet. The term is derived from the Italian word "cavallo," or horse: it metaphorically describes a horse galloping to the finish line.

Cadenza - A flourish or brilliant part of an aria (or concerto) commonly inserted just before a finale. It is usually performed without accompaniment.

Camerata - A gathering of Florentine writers and musicians between 1590 and 1600 who attempted to recreate what they believed was the ancient Greek theatrical synthesis of drama, music, and stage spectacle; their experimentation led to the creation of the early structural forms of modern opera.

Cantabile - An indication that the singer should sing sweetly.

Cantata - A choral piece generally containing Scriptural narrative texts: the *St. Matthew Passion* of Bach.

Cantilena - Literally, "little song." A lyrical melody meant to be played or sung "cantabile," or with sweetness and expression.

Canzone - A short, lyrical operatic song usually containing no narrative association with the drama but rather simply reflecting the character's state of mind: Cherubino's "Voi che sapete" in Mozart's *The Marriage of Figaro*.

Castrato - A young male singer who was surgically castrated to retain his treble voice.

Cavatina - A short aria popular in 18th and 19th century opera that usually heralded the entrance of a principal singer.

Classical Period - A period roughly between the Baroque and Romantic periods, the late 18th through the early 19th centuries. Stylistically, the music of the period stresses clarity, precision, and rigid structural forms.

Coda - A trailer added on by the composer after the music's natural conclusion. The coda serves as a formal closing to the piece.

Coloratura - Literally, "colored": it refers to a soprano singing in the bel canto tradition. It is a singing technique that requires great agility, virtuosity, embellishments and ornamentation: The Queen of the Night's aria, "Zum Leiden bin ich auserkoren," from Mozart's *The Magic Flute.*

Commedia dell'arte - A popular form of dramatic presentation originating in Renaissance Italy in which highly stylized characters were involved in comic plots involving mistaken identities and misunderstandings. Two of the standard characters were Harlequin and Colombine: The "play within a play" in Leoncavallo's *I Pagliacci.*

Comprimario - A singer who performs secondary character roles such as confidantes, servants, and messengers.

Continuo, Basso continuo - A bass part (as for a keyboard or stringed instrument) that was used especially in baroque ensemble music; it consists of an independent succession of bass notes that indicate the required chords and their appropriate harmonies. Also called *figured bass, thoroughbass.*

Contralto - The lowest female voice, derived from "contra" against, and "alto" voice; a voice between the tenor and mezzo-soprano.

Countertenor - A high male voice generally singing within the female high soprano ranges.

Counterpoint - The combination of two or more independent melodies into a single harmonic texture in which each retains its linear character. The most sophisticated form of counterpoint is the fugue form, in which from two to six melodies can be used; the voices are combined, each providing a variation on the basic theme but each retaining its relation to the whole.

Crescendo - A gradual increase in the volume of a musical passage.

Da capo - Literally, "from the top"; repeat. Early 17th-century da capo arias were in the form of A B A, with the second A section repeating the first, but with ornamentation.

Deus ex machina - Literally "god out of a machine." A dramatic technique in which a person or thing appears or is introduced suddenly and unexpectedly; it provides a contrived solution to an apparently insoluble dramatic difficulty.

Diatonic - A major or minor musical scale that comprises intervals of five whole steps and two half steps.

Diminuendo - Gradually becoming softer; the opposite of crescendo.

Dissonance - A mingling of discordant sounds that do not harmonize within the diatonic scale.

Diva - Literally, "goddess"; generally the term refers to a leading female opera star who either possesses, or pretends to possess, great rank.

Dominant - The fifth tone of the diatonic scale; in the key of C, the dominant is G.

Dramatic soprano or tenor - A voice that is powerful, possesses endurance, and is generally projected in a declamatory style.

Dramma giocoso - Literally, "amusing (or humorous) drama." An opera whose story combines both serious and comic elements: Mozart's *Don Giovanni.*

Falsetto - A lighter or "false" voice; an artificially-produced high singing voice that extends above the range of the full voice.

Fioritura - It., "flowering"; a flowering ornamentation or embellishment of the vocal line within an aria.

Forte, fortissimo - Forte (*f*) means loud; mezzo forte (*mf*) is fairly loud; fortissimo (*ff*) is even louder; additional *fff*'s indicate greater degrees of loudness.

Glissando - Literally, "gliding." A rapid sliding up or down the scale.

Grand opera - An opera in which there is no spoken dialogue and the entire text is set to music, frequently treating serious and tragic subjects. Grand opera flourished in France in the 19th century (Meyerbeer); the genre is epic in scale and combines spectacle, large choruses, scenery, and huge orchestras.

Heldentenor - A tenor with a powerful dramatic voice who possesses brilliant top notes and vocal stamina. Heldentenors are well suited to heroic (Wagnerian) roles: Lauritz Melchior in Wagner's *Tristan und Isolde.*

Imbroglio - Literally, "intrigue"; an operatic scene portraying chaos and confusion, with appropriate diverse melodies and rhythms.

Largo or larghetto - Largo indicates a very slow tempo, broad and with dignity. Larghetto is at a slightly faster tempo than largo.

Legato - Literally, "tied" or "bound"; successive tones that are connected smoothly. The opposite of legato is staccato (short and plucked tones.)

Leitmotif - Literally, "leading motive." A musical fragment characterizing a person, thing, feeling, or idea that provides associations when it recurs.

Libretto - Literally, "little book"; the text of an opera.

Lied - A German song; the plural is "lieder." Originally, a German art song of the late 18th century.

Lyric - A voice that is light and delicate.

Maestro - From the Italian "master"; a term of respect to conductors, composers, directors, and great musicians.

Melodrama - Words spoken over music. Melodrama appears in Beethoven's *Fidelio* and flourished during the late 19th century in the operas of Massenet (*Manon* and *Werther*).

Mezza voce - Literally, "medium voice"; singing with medium or half volume. It is sometimes intended as a vocal means to intensify emotion.

Mezzo-soprano - A woman's voice with a range between soprano and contralto.

Obbligato - An accompaniment to a solo or principal melody that is usually played by an important, single instrument.

Octave - A musical interval embracing eight diatonic degrees; from C to C is an octave.

Opera - Literally, "work"; a dramatic or comic play in which music is the primary vehicle that conveys its story.

Opera buffa - Italian comic opera that flourished during the bel canto era. Highlighting the opera buffa genre were buffo characters who were usually basses singing patter songs: Dr. Bartolo in Rossini's *The Barber of Seville*; Dr. Dulcamara in Donizetti's *The Elixir of Love.*

Opéra comique - A French opera characterized by spoken dialogue interspersed between the musical numbers, as opposed to grand opera in which there is no spoken dialogue. Opéra comique subjects can be either comic or tragic.

Operetta, or light opera - Operas that contain comic elements and generally a light romantic plot: Strauss's *Die Fledermaus*, Offenbach's *La Périchole*, and Lehar's *The Merry Widow.* In operettas, there is usually much spoken dialogue, dancing, practical jokes, and mistaken identities.

Oratorio - A lengthy choral work, usually of a religious nature and consisting chiefly of recitatives, arias, and choruses, but performed without action or scenery: Handel's *Messiah.*

Ornamentation - Extra embellishing notes—appoggiaturas, trills, roulades, or cadenzas—that enhance a melodic line.

Overture - The orchestral introduction to a musical dramatic work that sometimes incorporates musical themes within the work. Overtures are instrumental pieces that are generally performed independently of their respective operas in concert.

Parlando - Literally, "speaking"; the imitation of speech while singing, or singing that is almost speaking over the music. Parlando sections are usually short and have minimal orchestral accompaniment.

Patter song - A song with words that are rapidly and quickly delivered. Figaro's "Largo al factotum" in Rossini's *The Barber of Seville* is a patter song.

Pentatonic - A five-note scale. Pentatonic music is most prevalent in Far Eastern countries.

Piano - A performance indication for soft volume.

Pitch - The property of a musical tone that is determined by the frequency of the waves producing it.

Pizzicato - An indication that notes are to be played by plucking the strings instead of stroking the string with the bow.

Polyphony - Literally, "many voices." A style of musical composition in which two or more independent melodies are juxtaposed; counterpoint.

Polytonal - Several tonal schemes used simultaneously.

Portamento - A continuous gliding movement from one tone to another through all the intervening pitches.

Prelude - An orchestral introduction to an act or a whole opera that precedes the opening scene.

Presto, prestissimo - Vigorous, and with the utmost speed.

Prima donna - Literally, "first lady." The female star or principal singer in an opera cast or opera company.

Prologue - A piece sung before the curtain goes up on the opera proper: Tonio's Prologue in Leoncavallo's *I Pagliacci.*

Quaver - An eighth note.

Range - The span of tonal pitch of a particular voice: soprano, mezzo-soprano, contralto, tenor, baritone, and bass.

Recitative - A formal device used to advance the plot. It is usually sung in a rhythmically free vocal style that imitates the natural inflections of speech; it conveys the dialogue and narrative in operas and oratorios. *Secco*, or dry, recitative is accompanied by harpsichord and sometimes with other continuo instruments; *accompagnato* indicates that the recitative is accompanied by the orchestra.

Ritornello - A refrain, or short recurrent instrumental passage between elements of a vocal composition.

Romanza - A solo song that is usually sentimental; it is shorter and less complex than an aria and rarely deals with terror, rage, or anger.

Romantic Period - The Romantic period is usually considered to be between the early 19th and early 20th centuries. Romanticists found inspiration in nature and man. Von Weber's *Der Freischütz* and Beethoven's *Fidelio* (1805) are considered the first German Romantic operas; many of Verdi's operas as well as the early operas of Wagner are also considered Romantic operas.

Roulade - A florid, embellished melody sung to one syllable.

Rubato - An expressive technique, literally meaning "robbed"; it is a fluctuation of tempo within a musical phrase, often against a rhythmically steady accompaniment.

Secco - "Dry"; the type of accompaniment for recitative played by the harpsichord and sometimes continuo instruments.

Semitone - A half step, the smallest distance between two notes. In the key of C, the half steps are from E to F and from B to C.

Serial music - Music based on a series of tones in a chosen pattern without regard for traditional tonality.

Sforzando - Sudden loudness and force; it must stand out from the texture and be emphasized by an accent.

Singspiel - Literally, "song drama." Early German style of opera employing spoken dialogue between songs: Mozart's *The Magic Flute.*

Soprano - The highest range of the female voice ranging from lyric (light and graceful quality) to dramatic (fuller and heavier in tone).

Sotto voce - Literally, "below the voice"; sung softly between a whisper and a quiet conversational tone.

Soubrette - A soprano who sings supporting roles in comic opera: Adele in Strauss's *Die Fledermaus*; Despina in Mozart's *Così fan tutte.*

Spinto - From the Italian "spingere" (to push); a singer with lyric vocal qualities who "pushes" the voice to achieve heavier dramatic qualities.

Sprechstimme - Literally, "speaking voice." The singer half sings a note and half speaks; the declamation sounds like speaking but the duration of pitch makes it seem almost like singing.

Staccato - Short, clipped, detached, rapid articulation; the opposite of legato.

Stretto - Literally, "narrow." A concluding passage performed in a quick tempo to create a musical climax.

Strophe - Strophe is a rhythmic system of repeating lines. A musical setting of a strophic text is characterized by the repetition of the same music for all strophes.

Syncopation - A shifting of the beat forward or back from its usual place in the bar; a temporary displacement of the regular metrical accent in music caused typically by stressing the weak beat.

Supernumerary - A "super"; a performer with a non-singing and non-speaking role: "Spear-carrier."

Symphonic poem - A large orchestral work in one continuous movement, usually narrative or descriptive in character: Franz Liszt's *Les Preludes*; Richard Strauss's *Don Juan, Till Eulenspiegel,* and *Ein Heldenleben.*

Tempo - The speed at which music is performed.

Tenor - The highest natural male voice.

Tessitura - The usual range of a voice part.

Tonality - The organization of all the tones and harmonies of a piece of music in relation to a tonic (the first tone of its scale).

Tone poem - An orchestral piece with a program.

Tonic - The principal tone of the key in which a piece is written. C is the tonic of C major.

Trill - Two adjacent notes rapidly and repeatedly alternated.

Tutti - All together.

Twelve-tone - The twelve chromatic tones of the octave placed in a chosen fixed order and constituting, with some permitted permutations and derivations, the melodic and harmonic material of a serial musical piece. Each note of the chromatic scale is used as part of the melody before any other note is repeated.

Verismo - Literally “truth”; the artistic use of contemporary everyday material in preference to the heroic or legendary in opera. A movement particularly in Italian opera during the late 19th and early 20th centuries: Mascagni’s *Cavalleria rusticana.*

Vibrato - A “vibration”; a slightly tremulous effect imparted to vocal or instrumental tone to enrich and intensify sound, and add warmth and expressiveness through slight and rapid variations in pitch.

15972459R00065

Made in the USA
Middletown, DE
30 November 2014